FANNING THE SPARK

FANNING the SPARK

a memoir

MARY WARD BROWN

The University of Alabama Press • Tuscaloosa

The University of Alabama Press
Tuscaloosa, Alabama 35487-0380
uapress.ua.edu

Hardcover edition published 2009.
Paperback edition published 2016.
eBook edition published 2013.

Inquiries about reproducing material from this work should be addressed to the
University of Alabama Press.

Typeface: Minion Pro

Manufactured in the United States of America
Cover image: Relief engraving of Mary Ward Brown by Barry Moser
Cover design: Michele Myatt Quinn

∞
The paper on which this book is printed meets the minimum requirements of American
National Standard for Information Science–Permanence of Paper for Printed Library
Materials, ANSI Z39.48-1984.

Paperback ISBN: 978-0-8173-5866-2

A previous edition of this book has been catalogued by the Library of Congress as follows:
Library of Congress Cataloging-in-Publication Data
Brown, Mary Ward.
Fanning the spark : a memoir / Mary Ward Brown.
    p. cm.
ISBN 978-0-8173-1645-7 (cloth : alk. paper)—ISBN 978-0-8173-8154-7 (electronic)
1. Brown, Mary Ward. I. Title.
PS3552.R6944Z46   2009
813'.54—dc22
    [B]   2008029212

This book is for my granddaughters

MARY HAYS BROWN &
HELEN WARD BROWN

CONTENTS

ACKNOWLEDGMENTS

This memoir ends in 2003. A number of friends who have been an important part of my life and my work are not included in the tightly condensed narrative. Others, whom I hadn't met, or with whom I hadn't been closely connected at the time, are also not included. I wish to thank them here.

Bob and Clark Eiland
Bill Eiland and Andrew Ladis
Randall Curb
Winifred Cobbs
Norman and Joan McMillan
Annie Ford and Glynn Wheeler
Sterling and Jessie Haynes
Joe Hagood
Doug Halbrooks
Shane Lee
Lisa Griffin
Walter Givhan
Dan Gross
Scott Hereford
Betty Blackwell
Peggy Galis

In truth, I would like to thank everyone in the towns of Marion, Marion Junction, Greensboro, and Selma for their long support.

FANNING THE SPARK

1

CHILDHOOD

THE URGE TO WRITE must have smoldered in my makeup from the beginning, but my childhood did not ignite it.

My parents, with little formal schooling, had no interest in writing. They were doers. Born and raised in relatively poor Chilton County, Alabama, they moved in 1910 to Perry County, the then-prosperous Black Belt. From its owner-operator, they bought a large two-story general store in the Hamburg community, nine miles of unpaved road from Marion and twenty-one miles from Selma.

They lived first in the top floor of the store, a building so large the upstairs hall had first been used as a skating rink. As they prospered they bought land for cotton, row crops, and timber. My mother became the storekeeper/bookkeeper, while my father looked after what came to be, besides the farm, a cotton gin, dairy, grist mill, shop, blacksmith shop, and sawmill.

With roads all but impassable in wet weather, the village of Hamburg was basically self-sustaining. There were small stores other than my father's, a Post Office with postmistress, and a Methodist Church. The Southern Railroad ran through twice a day bringing mail and dry goods. In time my father shipped bales of cotton from the Hamburg station.

By the time I was born in 1917, my parents still lived in the top of the store, but a growing number of black people lived and worked on their land. My mother ran the store with the help of one black clerk, Bob Spencer, and kept all of the books. My father, unless dealing with salesmen up front, was out on the place or back in his office, the only room in the large open space of the store.

During all of my childhood, except on Sundays, both of my parents were already at work when I work up in the morning. Black people took care of me all day. My early childhood is a blur of long directionless days, followed about by various nurses. Like Topsy in Uncle Tom's Cabin, "I just growed." I could go and see my mother in the store whenever I liked, but she was usually busy with a customer.

Joanna Jackson, a black woman, was my mainstay during those early years. She was there before I was born and until I was grown and married. I was taught to call her Mammy as a necessary member of our family. "Mammy" is now considered demeaning, a reminder of servitude and oppression. For us it was a term of respect and affection, as for a surrogate mother or grandmother.

She was officially our cook. I had a succession of nurses, but she was the one in charge while my mother was at work downstairs. And she probably saved my life. As a toddler I was wasting away with colitis because no formula agreed with me. Mammy couldn't bear to see me pick up crumbs from the floor to eat out of hunger, so one day she slipped me a teaspoon of buttermilk. When it did no harm, she gave me more. By the time I was drinking a full cup and improving, she told my mother.

I once wrote a description of her lap. "If my mother ever sat and held me as a child I don't remember, but I do remember the solace of Mammy's lap. Though she was small, light-skinned, and far from the stereotype, her lap could spread and deepen to accommodate any wound. It smelled of gingham and a smoky cabin, and it rocked gently during tears. It didn't spill me out with token consolation but was there as long as needed. It was pure heartsease."

The previous owners of the store had sold coffins. Leftover black metal caskets were stacked halfway to the ceiling on one side of an unused room upstairs. The rest of the room was empty space. The Coffin Room, we called it, and I liked to play in there with my dolls and doll buggy. I put my dolls to sleep in the cheap caskets lined with yellowing white satin, and sometimes got in myself and lay down. I probably took a few naps in the coffins. I don't remember that a nurse was ever in there with me, but it was just off the big dining room, so Mammy could check on me from the kitchen.

In and around the family I was called Sister because of my two half-brothers. My mother, a young widow, had married my father, who was divorced. Each had a son seventeen years old at the time I was born. So William Ward and Sheldon Fitts, no kin to each other, were both blood brothers to me. I regret having to put one before the other, even to give their names.

Sheldon, my mother's son, whom I called simply Brother, was a football star at Georgia Military College in Milledgeville, Georgia, when I first became aware of him. Handsome and affectionate, his short visits home were as good as Santa's to me. Later, from the University of Georgia where he was an even greater star, he brought me a Little Sister Sigma Chi pin, which I lost playing in a pasture behind the store, and hunted for years without finding. And once he called to say he'd had an orchestra play "Sweetheart of Sigma Chi" for me at some event, probably a dance.

His football glory at the University was short lived, however, because of a knee injury. The university sent him to New York to a famous sports surgeon, but the injury couldn't be repaired. So he lost his football scholarship and went to work, first for the Coca-Cola Company.

In time, in Chicago, he earned a law degree in night school and married Frances Balhatchett, daughter of a Chicago surgeon. They had two children, Sheldon Jr. and a daughter, Barbara, who died tragically from a ruptured appendix at age eleven. Years later, they moved back to Hamburg and lived just down the road from me.

William Ward was usually known as Willie, but I followed the lead of his wife's sister who called him Brother Bill. He had a mind for business like our father and was already, when I first remember him, working in the Selma shoe store he was later to own. He was also already married to Sister Myrtle (Harrison). They came to visit on Sunday afternoons. Sister Myrtle had two diamonds in tall Tiffany settings inherited from her grandmothers, and I liked sitting beside her on the sofa, playing with her rings. All of our shoes came from Brother Bill's store.

Hurt no doubt by divorce, Brother Bill was less outwardly affectionate than Brother but equally as tenderhearted. His mother, "Miss Irene," my father's ex-wife, lived with him and Sister Myrtle all of her life. When my own mother died and our father remarried, Brother Bill invited me to come there whenever I liked, and I went from time to time. Miss Irene treated me as a member of the family, and I enjoyed going out with friends, to movies on my own, or reading in summer on their screened side porch beneath a large ceiling fan.

In addition to the shoe store, Brother Bill became a landowner like our father, whom he called Papa and I called Daddy. I think Brother Bill aspired to equal or outdo the parent who'd left him, and he did. But he enjoyed his success as our father never did. Brother Bill wore expensive suits and ties, drove good cars, took long summer vacations. When I was a teenager, he and Sister Myrtle took me to the beach in summer. In 1962 they took my son Kirtley Ward and me to the World's Fair in Seattle. For most of his life Brother Bill had kidney problems like our father, and lived for several years with one kidney. He died in 1964.

He and Sister Myrtle had no children so Kirtley Ward was one of his heirs. Kirtley Ward lives today on property, and in a house, inherited from his Uncle Bill.

Among my memories of the store, one has to do with a white farm overseer who had a drinking problem. In the memory, he whispered to me in a corner of the store, "Sister, go back there (behind the counter) and get me a bottle of lemon extract." I didn't think I was supposed to do it, or to let anyone know if I did, but I remember going and giving him the bottle. He drank it for the alcohol content, I was to find out in time.

Another store memory is of sliding back doors to the candy counter and taking out a handful of Hershey's kisses, silver-wrapped then as now. Peeled and packed into one side of my jaw, they melted slowly, deliciously. I don't think this was forbidden since I did it often, with cavities to show for it later.

One indelible store memory is of my mother, sitting at a home-made wooden table with heavy account books spread out before her. As she pulled down the lever to a large black adding machine on her right, she was silently weeping. When she looked up to see me she attempted to straighten her face, caught my small body, and hugged me fiercely to her.

My mother had heavy responsibilities. Besides her work in the store, she was responsible for our living quarters upstairs and for two children, one away from home. Upstairs she had a cook and someone to clean, but she never knew who or how many would be at our table for "dinner," as southerners called the main meal of the day served at noon. Two rural schoolteachers lived and boarded with us. One farm overseer ate with us regularly, plus any salesman, county agent, dairy inspector, or anyone else who happened

With my mother, Hamburg, 1917.

to be in the store on business at the noon hour. Salesmen, called drummers, ate with us on a regular basis. There was Roy Carter day, Cecil Kynard day, Mr. Cox day.

In summer my mother supervised a season-long canning operation upstairs. Hundreds of jars of fruits, vegetables, pickles, and preserves were put up in our kitchen. They helped feed us in winter, were shared with my brothers, and used as gifts for friends. In winter, hogs were killed, the fresh meat cooked, and by-products made into sauce meat. Hams, and sausages packed in casings, were prepared for the smokehouse out back. My mother was running up and down the stairs all day.

She kept a flock of turkeys for holiday dinners, ours, those of my brothers, certain friends and drummers. Brother's turkeys, in homemade wooden crates supplied with grain and water, went by train to Chicago. The turkeys hadn't sense enough to get out of the rain and would stand in a downpour with their heads up and drown. My mother had to run out in boots and raincoat to put them up.

Feeling overwhelmed no doubt, on the day of my memory, she must have looked up to see me and thought, "And *you,* my neglected baby!"

Some of the happiest times of my childhood were spent with the Lee family who lived across the pasture. Mrs. Lee was a musician who gave me piano lessons. I had no talent but learned to sight-read well enough to finally play hymns for the Hamburg Church. And after lessons I could stay and play with her six children. In their large front yard we played baseball and games such as Red Light and Slinging Statues. In the house we played charades and card games. In summer Mrs. Lee took us swimming in the Hamburg community swimming pool, and in the fall nutting in the woods for hickory nuts and chinquapins.

After I'd grown up, someone said to me one day, "You always walked with your head down when you were little." We hadn't known that I was nearsighted until I was tested in school. Finally fitted with glasses, I wouldn't wear them out of vanity. For years I was putting them on, taking them off, losing them, and trying to find more becoming frames in ever changing styles, big, little, wire, plastic.

I still remember one strong *feeling* about my early years. I didn't like walking barefoot in the black prairie mud, and I didn't want the soupy muck squishing up between my toes. I wanted to be somewhere else at the time, I remember, somewhere I thought of as *nice.*

And later, when I began trying to write fiction, I read with great admiration the work of Katherine Anne Porter (*Flowering Judas; The Leaning Tower; Pale Horse, Pale Rider*). Her claims of growing up in fine houses, tall secretaries filled with leather-bound classics, made me feel deprived. I could be a better writer, I thought, if I'd grown up in such surroundings.

But after Porter's death, her biographer, Joan Givner, brought to light that she'd grown up in poverty, her early years without certain needs, much less luxuries. This impressed me even more with her accomplishment. I saw what genius can do with a given material, even deprivation and dreams.

And it made me face a truth of my own. I did not have genius and, if I intended to write, would have to make do with the ability I had. I wasn't even sure that what I had was talent, and not simply a strong desire and will to write.

2

SCHOOL

SCHOOL CHANGED MY LIFE with books and learning. I went first to the Black Belt Consolidated Academy, grades one through five, a few miles from Hamburg. There were two teachers, two rooms, and a cloakroom.

I don't remember learning to read, only that the world began to widen out from the one that I knew, and doors seemed to open in the skull of my head. I was enchanted by my readers, with their stories of the Little Red Hen and her seed, of Big Billy Goat Gruff and the Troll.

At home there were newspapers and farm magazines but no books except the Bible, which I never tried to read. There must have been a few children's books of some kind, as evidenced by an early snapshot with my father on the store porch, but I don't remember them. I do remember looking forward to a magazine subscription such as *Child Craft*, to which I submitted a poem and received a rejection in the mail.

In the Methodist Church behind our house, attended by everyone in the community (my parents were Baptist), there was a book titled *The Devil in Society* or *Palaces of Sin*. It had pictures of women in bloomers kicking up their legs in a chorus line, and of the devil himself with his pitchfork. I brought it home to read but found it no more understandable than the Bible. Years later, when

With my father
on the porch of
the store.

an interviewer asked what books I read as a child, the only title I
could think of was that one.

After skipping a grade, I went to junior high school in Marion on the schoolbus and discovered, or uncovered, a lasting love
for literature. In the school library I found and read *Lord Jim* by
Joseph Conrad, in which I was somehow able to recognize good
writing. Conrad didn't remain a favorite, but I remember being excited by the discovery that writing can be good enough to be read
again and again, over years, good enough to be art, the meaning

of which I could only intuit at the time. Afterwards, I was always looking for that quality in the books that I read.

And I came to look upon literature as a friend. It was my nature to like people, so I always had friends. But friendships are subject to change, even heartbreak. My high school boyfriend with the sun-bleached blonde hair moved away and out of my life. My brilliant college roommate developed schizophrenia and turned against me as a member of "the plot."

But literature was always there with fact or fiction. A good book could take me from problems of my own to those of Emma Bovary or Anna Karenina, to Ahab and his long pursuit of the Great White Whale, to Gandhi and his amazing *Autobiography: The Story of My Experiments with Truth.*

There was only one time when literature couldn't help. When my husband died, I couldn't read fiction for more than a year. Finally a short story, "The Boat," by Alistair MacLeod of Nova Scotia, caught and held my attention. I was so grateful that I wrote and thanked the author. "The Boat" is still one of my favorite short stories, the author one of my favorite writers.

I loved my high school English books, loved writing themes, and soon began writing for the school paper, *The Perri-Winkle* (Perry County High School). During my second year as editor, *The Perri-Winkle* won second place in a statewide contest sponsored by the Alabama Polytechnic Institute (Auburn University) School of Journalism. My letter from Professor Joseph E. Roop, March 20, 1934, said in part, "I think you can well be proud of having defeated the papers from such large schools as Phillips and Ensley in Birmingham. Better luck next year."

Doing well in high school was easy, because I wanted to learn and liked to study. My schoolbooks were not thrown around, dogeared, or allowed to get wet, though I felt free to underline pages with a pencil if I made the lines straight. And I set myself to do each daily assignment. When not attuned to a subject such as trigonometry, I simply memorized it.

My parents had built, while I was in grammar school, a modest house next door to the store. So I had a quiet room of my own and studied by the light of a kerosene Aladdin lamp. The house plan they chose was from a book featuring the American Bungalow, an awkward style popular in the nineteen twenties. Our house had two stories instead of one, and one redeeming feature: All of the interior walls were of heart pine saved from my father's sawmill. A sleeping porch was added later and the breakfast room enlarged. It's the house that I live in today, still with only one bathroom. Upstairs.

When I came home from school on the schoolbus each day, I rode my horse, Palo, for a while, ate the supper Mammy left out covered over with a clean white cloth, and did homework until bedtime.

My report cards were seldom signed more than three or four times during a school year. Both of my parents looked at them with pride, I think, but hadn't time at the moment to sign them. I still have a high school report card with almost solid A+'s, signed four times in my father's rushed, run-together signature, T. I. Ward. His name was Thomas Ira. My mother's name was Mary, so I was named for both, Mary Thomas.

It didn't seem unusual to me that my report cards were seldom signed, and it wasn't questioned by my teachers. I never felt neglected or unappreciated, and I always knew that I was loved. In truth, my parents were providing for me then, and until this day, when I live in the house they built and on the land they left to support me. I could never have survived on my income from writing.

In 1934 I entered Judson College in nearby Marion as a boarding student. I'd wanted to go away to a university, preferably South Carolina where I had several friends, but my mother was diagnosed with uterine cancer after my last year of high school. So my parents' college plan for me was, I think, to have me close to home.

I didn't do well at Judson as I had in high school. At home I'd studied alone in a quiet place. Now there were girls in every room, some ready to talk, smoke against the rules as I learned to do the first week, drink Coca-Colas and eat Hershey bars until midnight. I couldn't resist this secondary education. My first report cards with C's, an occasional D, shocked me. Still, I didn't buckle down and make the Dean's List until my junior year.

I knew that my mother was seriously sick. But I didn't think she would die, partly because I was young and death had no reality for me, and also because she shielded me from the truth. Her primary wish for me at the time, I think, was that I should get through school and be "educated," as she felt she was not. So I lived at Judson with sporadic weekends at home, and was sent to Alabama College, Montevallo, for two summers, supposedly to get off requirements and help with editing the school paper. My mother died during my junior year. I was eighteen.

The local newspaper account of her funeral reads, in part:

> Services for Mrs. T. I. Ward, 55, held at 2 o'clock Sunday afternoon at her home at Hamburg, were attended by several hundred sorrowing friends from throughout this section. . . .
>
> In the sorrowing throng paying a last tribute to Mrs. Ward were all the colored servants and workers of the Ward plantation, and at the conclusion of the service for this beloved woman some 50 of the Negroes sang two of her favorite spirituals.

After her death, I learned that when she knew her time was short, she made an appointment with Miss Bessie Welch, Dean of Residence and Professor of English at Judson. She had herself driven to the appointment by Hamp Lee, Daddy's driver, and told Miss Welch of her condition. As she left she said, "Please look after my little girl."

Miss Welch didn't tell me of the visit until I was out of school, but she did look after me. I was always aware of her watchful concern, and I went to her room many nights for comfort and advice.

But I have never forgiven myself for not helping my mother, whom I called Mama, through her long ordeal, which must have been lonely. Now, when I feel a sometime lack of concern from my own little family, I remind myself of my own neglect and of the old truism "what goes around comes around," and of the Buddhist maxim "Everything I do always comes back to me."

I was relatively untouched by the Great Depression. My parents had worked so hard without thought for luxuries or pleasure that I assumed we were poor, only slightly better off than the black people on the place. So I was surprised to find that most of my Judson friends and classmates had to help pay their tuition by waiting on tables, doing secretarial work or other extra-curricular jobs.

I was graduated in 1938 without awards or honors. But I'd faithfully edited the school paper, *The Triangle*, for two years. With the help of a small staff, I'd brought it out on schedule, and we'd personally handed out copies each month as students came from the dining hall after Saturday night dinner. Saturday night dinners were formal at the time, often with a program, evening dress required. I saved a letter from Dean R. A. McLemore, dated May 22, 1937.

Dear Editor,

I would like to express to you and your staff my deep appreciation for your splendid work this semester. It is my belief that we have had the best paper in the history of Judson College. . . . I desire especially to congratulate you upon the regularity with which the paper has appeared.

I was graduated in the Centennial Class, the year Judson celebrated its hundredth birthday. Sixty years later, in a speech for a Judson financial campaign, I told of my personal experience.

I've tried to remember the big celebration that I know took place that year, but I can't come up with much. What I did remember was that I was graduating and didn't have any presents.

The beds of my classmates were covered with boxes of kid gloves, purses, Toujour Moi perfume, slips, and pajamas. Ribbons and tissue paper were everywhere.

But I hadn't sent out invitations. It would be asking for presents, I thought. Also, my mother had died and my father had remarried and, subconsciously, I probably wanted to keep a low profile. So there I was in my cap and gown without a single present.

But I'd been editor of the school paper, *The Triangle*, for two years, first as a junior and again as a senior. It was my college mission, I thought. It was printed at the shop of the *Marion Times Standard*, a weekly paper still published in Marion.

As we were about to go into the auditorium to get our diplomas, the editor and the linotypist of the *Marion Times* walked up in their Sunday clothes. I'd never seen them dressed up before. Sixty years ago, type was set and handled by hand, so the hands and clothes of everyone around a newspaper shop were usually covered with printer's ink.

But they had come, all cleaned up, to hand me a little box. Inside, they'd taken from the masthead of *The Triangle* the two-year-old, ink-blackened slug with my name and position on the staff, Editor-In-Chief. Beneath it, they'd put 30. Thirty was the journalistic symbol for the end of a news story or, broadly speaking, for the end of anything, such as my tenure at *The Triangle*. Below that, in bright new lines of type like a metal calling card, they'd added a message. "From all of us, in memory of a very pleasant business association. Congratulations and good luck." They'd taped it all together and put it in the little box. They brought a present too, a pen and pencil set, which hasn't survived.

But I've kept and treasured the type in the box all these years. It was the nicest thing anyone could have done for me that day, and I graduated happy like everybody else. Later I did get a Royal Portable typewriter from my father, an Elgin watch from one of my brothers, and other nice things.

And I'd taken a course in journalism, which set newspaper work as my career choice. I'd always been drawn to words as some are drawn to musical instruments, but journalism was the only form of wordplay to which I'd been exposed. Writing fiction had never occurred to me. So I applied for a scholarship to the Medill School of Journalism, Northwestern University, Evanston, Illinois, with the following result.

Dear Miss Ward:

Our Committee on Scholarships wishes to congratulate you on the general excellence of your application for a graduate scholarship but regrets that it is unable at this time to give you an appointment for 1939–1940.

I do not want you to feel discouraged over the fact that you were not selected. We had an unusually large number of strong applications this year (102 to be exact), many from men who have had considerably more newspaper experience than you. It is much to your credit that you placed as high in the list as you did considering the competition which you faced.

We want you to know that we shall be glad to accept you for graduate work and to admit you to candidacy for your master's degree, for we believe you are the type of student we want. . . . We shall do everything we can to help you find part-time work to finance your study here. . . . If you can raise enough money to finance part of your way, we can perhaps help you to earn the rest.

I don't remember that I was greatly disappointed. Like most college women of the nineteen-thirties I looked forward to marriage, a home, and children. In the same Campaign Judson speech, I wrote,

In my day, our unspoken goal was to get married, if possible, and have a family. When I was asked to be here tonight, it was suggested that I tell you what Judson had meant in my own life. One of the first things I thought of was that it helped me get a good husband, right off the bat. . . . (My husband had a particular connection to the college through his mother.)

As it turned out, just as I was graduating the journalism teacher who had so encouraged me, Miss Mae Brunson, was leaving to get her Master's degree. So I was given her job, with the lofty title, Publicity Director. I moved across the street from the dormitory to a house called Teachers' Cottage. And, so far as I remember, began work then and there.

"Publicity Director,"
Judson College, 1938.

I wrote college news for the daily papers, sent routine personal items about students to hometown papers, and wrote what features I could discover or uncover. I taught one class of freshman English, and struggled with the mechanics of two cameras that came with the publicity job.

And the year moved on to February. On Valentine's Day I was called to the phone in the downstairs lobby.

The caller said that he was Kirtley Brown of the Auburn News Bureau, that he was calling to tell me of an American College Publicity Association meeting to be held in New Orleans for three days, beginning April 10. He said that several publicity agents from the state were going and that the plan was to meet in Montgomery and drive down. He asked if I'd be interested in making the trip. I said that I would need permission from my boss, Dr. Leroy Cleverdon, the Judson president.

Mr. Brown went on to say that his mother was a Judson graduate of the eighteen-eighties, that she'd loved the school so much, in fact, that she'd named him for a favorite teacher, Miss Anne Elizabeth Kirtley. I was able to tell him that Miss Kirtley was still on campus, emeritus now, with blue hair, correcting us daily not to say "Hello, Miss Kirtley," but "Good morning" or "Good afternoon," like ladies.

Dr. Cleverdon encouraged me to go, and said the school would pay my expenses. In preparation, I went on a shopping spree to Birmingham (financed by Daddy, as he would find out later), and bought new shoes, a spring hat, and stylish long dress for the scheduled banquet.

On the appointed day I went by bus to Montgomery, where I was met by Kirtley Brown. He was a little older than I expected, but impressed me as a very nice man. He took me to the designated meeting place, *The Paragon Press*, where Ed Wise, the company president, was also going. No other publicists were there except Charles Dobbins from Alabama College, Montevallo (now the University of Montevallo). The two women who'd planned to go had dropped out.

My father had told me beforehand that if no other women were going, I shouldn't go down alone in a car with strange men. Kirtley, quick to appreciate my embarrassment, volunteered to go with me on the train. Ed and Charlie decided they might as well join us, so the four of us went to New Orleans on the day coach.

Ed and Charlie were married, but we went as a group to scheduled meetings and events, and to unscheduled nights in the French Quarter. From the beginning, I appreciated Kirtley's concern for me, the unsophisticated female in the foursome. And all of us enjoyed his spontaneous wit and good-humored attitude. Put to a vote, he would doubtless have been the group favorite.

But he and I didn't pair off until the long train ride home. As we boarded the train, he asked to share my seat. We were all exhausted, so Ed and Charlie went immediately to sleep in the seat behind us, but Kirtley and I stayed awake, talking. Perhaps exhaustion made us less guarded, more easily confidential. In any case, we talked all the way home, which was all night.

Sixty-seven days later, an Associated Press news release tells the rest of the story.

Mary T. Ward Will Be Bride of Kirtley Brown.

Marion, Ala.—(AP)—In working for "dear old alma mater," two young enterprising college publicity directors, Miss Mary T. Ward of Judson, and Kirtley Brown of Auburn, agreed today they had done pretty well by themselves.

They announced to friends they would be wed Sunday in the college chapel here, with Dr. L. G. Cleverdon, Judson president, officiating.

When the American College Publicity Association met at New Orleans in April, Auburn (Alabama Polytechnic Institute) sent Brown as its representative and Miss Ward was the delegate for Judson, noted college for young women on the opposite side of the state.

The two met at the convention. Romance grew apace.

Judson loses its publicity director, for the Browns will make their home in Auburn.

So we were married in the Judson College chapel, two months after we met, on my twenty-second birthday (Kirtley was thirty-six). And after a three-day Depression honeymoon in Montgomery, I went to Auburn as a bride.

With Kirtley in New Orleans. Photo by street photographer.

Old hotel receipt from honeymoon.

3

MARRIAGE

WE LIVED THAT FIRST SUMMER in the Kappa Delta Sorority apartment, which was one big room, a small kitchen, and room-sized screened porch. It was my introduction to cooking and housekeeping, about which I knew nothing (at home there was Mammy, with Classie and William to clean) and to college-town social life.

"Calling" was a custom in Auburn in the nineteen-thirties. After 3:30 in the afternoon, ladies of the town, in hats and white gloves, began paying fifteen-minute visits to newcomers in the community. It was a gesture of welcome, a way to become acquainted, perhaps to satisfy curiosity. It was a custom I'd never heard of. So the first callers found me in old shorts, worn out from cooking and housekeeping misadventures, sometimes asleep on the couch. If I didn't get to the door or wasn't at home, I found calling cards in the mailbox. And I learned from my sister-in-law, Sarah Brown, wife of Kirtley's brother Roberts, an Auburn attorney, that I was expected to return the calls. Which, once initiated, I tried to do.

When the KD's returned in the fall, we had to leave the apartment, so we moved, at the invitation of Kirtley's parents, to live with them in the antebellum house they'd bought and partially restored, three miles from town on Shelton Mill Road. The house, built in 1854, now known as Noble Hall, is included in *Ante-Bellum Mansions of Alabama* by Ralph Hammond.

The newlyweds, Auburn, 1939. Photo by Lewis Arnold, Kirtley's student photographer, later a professional photographer with a studio in Birmingham.

Kirtley's father, James Vandiver Brown, an Auburn alumnus and early football star, had been for years Superintendent of Buildings and Grounds. It was his custom to have two or three college boys live upstairs in the house and work part-time on the house and grounds in return for room and board. They were known as Dr. Brown's boys.

Kirtley and I lived upstairs across the wide central hall from the boys, with whom we shared a bathroom. Our big front room had floor-to-ceiling windows and a balcony where Kirtley and I sometimes slept on hot summer nights. Both of Kirtley's parents were dedicated gardeners, and, though they couldn't afford expensive inside restorations, the grounds were beautiful with a pleasant view from our windows.

My mother-in-law had a fulltime cook, and all of us ate together, three meals a day, in the large main dining room downstairs.

When Kirtley left for work each morning, I had nothing to do except keep our room straight and read. I read several tomes by Thomas Wolfe, on whom I had a literary crush at the time, and read so much that I tired of reading. I don't know why I didn't try to write, especially since I'd found that one of my new sisters-in-law, Margery Finn Brown, wife of Kirtley's brother Travis, an Army officer with whom she was away on assignment, was an aspiring writer. Her stories were later published in magazines such as *McCall's, Redbook, The Saturday Evening Post.*

But I liked clothes and, since we had no money to buy them, asked to use my mother-in-law's old sewing machine. We got it out, oiled it up, and I began learning to sew.

If I accepted an invitation to a morning coffee or luncheon in town, I had to stay the whole day. If I went simply to go, I'd have the whole morning, lunch with Kirtley, than wait until he finished work, often late. I felt welcome in the homes of friends, but didn't want to wear out my welcome, so spent the time looking for patterns and material, browsing through stores, mainly Burton's Book Store and the library.

I don't know how long this lasted, one year or two, when one morning I went to town with Kirtley. I don't remember what I did all day, only that he met me after work for supper and a movie.

The movie, entirely erased by what happened, didn't engross me from the start. All that I remember is a plague of grasshoppers eating up everything in sight on the screen. A loud humming and whirring filled the dark theatre.

And for the first time in my life, except after exercise, I felt the beating of my own heart. The beats became stronger, faster, and I began to be uneasy. Soon I could feel beats in my ears, the hollow of my throat. They began to skip, stop for an instant, and return with a thud that seemed to shake my whole body. Finally they were going so fast they seemed to be running together and I found it hard to breathe. I forgot where I was, forgot everything except the turmoil in my chest. I told Kirtley I was having a heart attack, and we rushed outside.

The doctor I'd chosen, and had visited earlier, met us in his office. He listened to my chest, front, back, up, down, low on both sides, then took off his stethoscope and smiled. There was nothing wrong with my heart, he said. It was a good heart and would last fifty more years at least.

"Forget your heart," he said. "Go home and get some sleep."

So we went home and to bed, but I didn't go to sleep. And I couldn't forget my heart. I didn't believe what the doctor had said. I thought he was mistaken, because no one else had wild, erratic beatings. And if they did no one knew, because they simply died. Would I die too?

And what then?, I tried to imagine. I didn't believe in heaven and hell. So would I be blotted out and simply not *be*? My mind reeled away from the thought and I lay frozen in horror before the prospect of total, endless, nothingness. Would day, night, people walking the streets, everything, continue as if I'd never lived at all?

Palpitations returned the next day, and the next. I couldn't sleep, couldn't eat, was afraid to be alone, to die alone. I became bone thin. My eyes in the mirror were like those of a trapped animal. People looked at me and looked away.

I was diagnosed with an acute anxiety neurosis. Today the symptoms are called panic attacks, and in the Age of Anxiety are more common, more easily treated with drugs unknown at the time.

We saw doctors in other places, other states, and I didn't improve. Finally we turned to Kirtley's relative, Dr. Stewart D. Brown, in Royston, Georgia. He put me in the small hospital he owned and operated at the time (it was later enlarged and endowed by his boyhood friend, Ty Cobb, as the Ty Cobb Health Center). They fed me good food, saw that I slept at night. And he talked to me, asked questions. Finally he advised us to move back to town and start a family.

So we rented half of a duplex apartment near the heart of town. I found that the attacks came less often, and could sometimes be aborted, if my attention was focused on something of interest. So I enrolled in a creative writing class, a large class of undergraduates. We were given impromptu writing exercises in class, speed-writing that I'd never liked, but no writing assignments.

So I soon dropped out and began trying to write stories at home. They were fragments of my own experience injected into supposedly fictional characters, a common practice of beginners. To learn that fiction is a product of the imagination, and not palmed-off personal experience, takes time and many failures.

By now, 1942, the country was at war with both Germany and Japan. Everyone was affected, young and old, men and women. Kirtley, though a little above draft age, had been classified 1A but not yet called. So he took on an additional job for the Navy. His brother Roberts (called Bob) was a glider pilot in England, his brother Travis a West Point graduate, was somewhere overseas.

I wanted to do more than knit mittens, so took a job as typist for a wartime engineering training program, the ESMWT. I worked in a large room with several other women, whom I came to know and enjoy. I felt good going to work and being part of the war effort, so I worked there until I became pregnant and afflicted with morning sickness.

My pregnancy was healthy and happy. I made baby clothes and

my own hospital gowns, walked each afternoon, and had no panic attacks that I remember.

But three months before the birth, my father died of renal failure. He knew that a grandchild was on the way, since I'd visited him, six months pregnant, in the hospital. But he never knew he'd have a grandson, which would have greatly pleased him.

From the *Opelika Daily News*, the following:

> Mr. and Mrs. Kirtley Brown, of Auburn, announce the birth of a son on December 24th at Drake Infirmary, Auburn, weighing six pounds, twelve ounces, who has been named Kirtley Ward Brown. Mrs. Brown was the former Mary Thomas Ward. Mr. Brown is the popular and efficient Director of Publicity and Publications for Auburn College.

In his will, my father left me the house, the store, and fifteen hundred of the three thousand acres of land he'd acquired. The rest went to my brothers, a small portion to my cousin, Ralph Eagle, a kind of third brother, who'd lived with us and worked with Daddy since his graduation from high school.

My land was located in and around Hamburg, with four hundred acres on the Cahaba River. The inheritance was to complicate and change the course of our lives.

Back from the hospital with my new baby, I had a cervical infection that wouldn't heal, and all of my old anxieties plus a new one. If I died or went crazy, who would take care of my baby!

Ralph, with Kirtley's participation from Auburn, agreed to take over management of my land and the store. But the entire area was in a state of flux, from farming to beef cattle. Ralph, who'd always liked horses, had started a business of his own with quarter horses, the breed used to handle cattle. So his hands were already full.

Kirtley, meanwhile, had been made Auburn's first Director of Student Affairs or Dean of Men. So he had a new job, new baby, and the responsibility of a sick wife's inheritance.

His new job in Auburn was stressful. It was his duty to tell a father that his son had been expelled for cheating. He was called out in the middle of the night because of a campus melee. A student was killed in an automobile accident. It was up to Kirtley to collect details and, with his new father's heart, call the parents. He brought a pregnant girl to our house (we'd moved to a larger place) before her dismissal.

So his frequent weekend trips to confer with Ralph in Hamburg, a complete change of pace and place, may have been less hard on him than it seemed at the time. Ralph's wife, Martha, graciously took him into their home while he was there.

But after four years, he made the decision that if we intended to keep the land, we should move back and live on it. I remember not being thrilled to go back to the country and the prairie mud. But, sick or well, I could never have given it up. My parents had worked too hard for it.

Kirtley and Kirtley Ward, before our return to Hamburg.

4

RETURN TO HAMBURG

KIRTLEY WARD (KW from now on) was four when we moved back to the farm. Allen Jones, a black boy, aged eleven, who'd been raised on the place, came up for a pittance to look after and play with him each morning. Mammy's daughters, Nannie and Betty, were here to help me. Mammy was still living but retired to her house, her potted plants, and her puttering.

Ralph had already begun our transition from row crops to cattle. Ralph was a born cattleman, and had brought the first quarter horse stallion to Alabama. Later, in 1981, he was inducted into the Alabama Livestock Hall of Fame.

Kirtley had never lived on a farm, much less managed one. But with the help of K. G. Baker, director of the Auburn University Experiment Station at nearby Marion Junction, and with help from the entire Auburn Agriculture Department (he'd worked at Auburn for seventeen years), he became a good cattleman.

He liked the out-of-doors, the cows, and all the farm animals, including KW's goat, Bosco. He liked wearing cowboy boots and being his own boss, and he enjoyed our individualistic country neighbors. But I always wondered if, and how much, he missed the college campus where he'd seemed so much to belong.

In working on this memoir I found a small blue envelope that said in bold black print, "Your Passport To Successful Writing."

Inside, dated August 27, 1946, was the result of a Writing Aptitude Test I'd taken from some long-forgotten commercial advertisement. "There is splendid general equipment here, including real talent," someone had written. All that I needed, the person wrote, was to sign up for their program, price not stated.

So I must have thought, at least, of trying to write, now that I was back in the country. It would be a while before I did anything about it.

I remember certain rainy days when Allen couldn't come and KW couldn't go outside. We'd open all the downstairs doors, living room, dining room, breakfast room, den. I'd play "The Happy Farmer" on our old Chickering piano, and he'd ride his tricycle round and round through all of the rooms. At times he'd lean over the handlebars and go full speed while I played fast and loud. Then he'd slow down to waltz time, and I'd follow until the next change of pace. He'd change routes, carefully avoiding furniture, then reverse the change. Neither of us spoke during those races. He'd ride and I'd play until he gave out and the game was over.

Since he was born on Christmas Eve and couldn't start school at six, and since no kindergarten was available, I decided to prepare him for school by the Calvert School method. I set up a schoolroom on the sleeping porch, with a teacher's desk and fresh flower in a bud vase. But he wasn't ready to put his mind on letters and numbers, and kept looking out the windows for Allen.

Our neighbor's preschool daughter, Shirley Crawford, though, came to visit one day and was fascinated. Back in the car with her mother, she looked at the big print on a magazine cover, pointed to a letter, and said, "That's a B."

So we gave up and stored the Calvert School material upstairs in Daddy's old store, where it moldered for years.

Above: With Mammy, retired, in her front yard.

Right: Kirtley W. and Allen Jones on top of the house they built in our back yard.

We never tried to run the store. Ralph leased it for a while to a retired uncle, then to an old friend, who gave it a try. But roads were paved by then and people shopped in town. The building stood empty for years, home of rats and varmints. Our fire insurance was cancelled, and in 1969 while KW was out of the country, we sold it for the lumber. He never forgave us, since he'd once had a dark room in the bathroom upstairs, and had studied for his bar exam in Daddy's old office. But we saved the old pine shelves, now bookcases in the library of his home.

Still handicapped by neurosis, I was afraid to be alone, to be in crowds, to drive the car. All of us were worn out with my problems. I spent a week in Hillcrest, a psychiatric hospital in Birmingham, which didn't help. So during the summer before KW was to enter his first grade of school, I was sent to Touro Infirmary in New Orleans for electric shock therapy. It was meant to change the patterns of my thinking.

The practice was new, the procedure fearsome. I was told to step on a low stool, then climb, unsedated and fully aware, onto a high table where I was strapped down and my mouth stuffed with towels to prevent biting my tongue. The prescribed jolt of electricity sent my body into convulsions. I knew nothing until I was back in my room, where I opened my eyes to a total blank, a tabula rasa. I didn't know where I was and, most unsettling of all, I didn't know *who* I was. Memory came back by degrees, always ending in a flood of tears. What on earth was to become of me!

I was given five shock treatments. During one, a vertebra in my backbone was injured, which started the arthritis that I have today. And while I was there, it was decided to surgically remove by conization the cervical infection that had never healed completely.

Back home, we'd come to know a retired Army doctor, Colonel

William T. Weissinger, who carried on a limited medical practice from two back rooms of the antebellum house in which he and his wife had settled. He gave me vitamin B12 shots once a week for a long period of time. He also gave advice such as "working off your nerves." Scrub a floor, weed a flower bed, iron a shirt, he said. So I began to improve physically, but still lived under a cloud of depression.

Psychology had been my minor at Judson, so I'd been reading Freud and Jung, anyone I though might help, but I'd resisted the field of religion. Finally, out of desperation, I decided to read again, not familiar parts, but the entire Four Gospels of the New Testament. This time I understood that Jesus was teaching a special way to live. He gave his followers a New Commandment, to simply love one another. But the love He commanded had teeth. In my case, it would call for a change of focus, away from myself and my miseries to something other and bigger.

Within the family, I'd been thinking, "Why don't you understand me and make me happy?" When I tried to think, "Why don't I understand you and make you happy?" the dynamics changed. An about-face was required of me, toward anyone, everyone, anywhere.

I didn't think I could change without support, so we joined the Episcopal Church because we liked the beauty and confines of the ritual. And my neurosis began to leave like an evil spirit. Not all at once, but completely. Looking back, it seems a small latter-day miracle.

In retrospect I think I understand a little of what caused my neurosis. I wasn't being challenged to use all of my powers. And, settled into marriage and the future, I faced an unconscious philosophical question, simply put in a song made famous by Peggy Lee, "Is that all there is?" The lyrics go on to say, "If that's all there is, my friends, let's keep on dancing. Let's bring out the booze, and have a ball, if that's all there is."

Years later I was asked in a written interview, "What is your view of the afterlife? Did this affect how you approached stories like "Disturber of the Peace" or "Goodbye, Cliff"?

My answer:

"When I was around twenty-three years old, I became obsessed with a fear of death. What I feared most was to be blotted out, to lose consciousness and personal identity forever.

But later on our farm, I watched the birth of a calf. The calf came out in a package like Saran-wrap from the grocery store. I have never seen such perfect packaging or economy. When the package was on the ground, the cow licked it open, and the little calf stood up on wobbly legs, nudged around the mother's flank until it found what it was meant to find, and began to nurse. Both mother and calf knew exactly what to do. It was the most awe-inspiring sight I have seen to this day. It somehow put to rest my worst fears about death. If birth could be so right and good, then death must be too, I decided."

Farming was now behind us. We were raising grade Hereford beef cattle. The pastures were lush with crimson clover, White Dutch clover, and Caley peas. The cows were fat and pricey. When I say *we* I should say *he*, because Kirtley looked after the place and all of the business, while I, unlike my mother, could be a housewife.

Healthy at last, I enjoyed my job. Mammy's daughter, Nannie, had come to cook. I'd learned to cook as well by then, so both of us spent our mornings in the kitchen. This was what most middle-class southern women did at the time. Our main meal, served in the middle of the day, was called dinner. Working men in town as well as in the country came home to eat.

I was a recipe cook, not one of the gifted, but Nannie and I worked together, learning from each other. Each day we cooked meat or chicken, at least two fresh vegetables, made salads (sometimes congealed), hot bread (cornbread, bicuits, yeast rolls or bread; I especially liked kneading dough and baking bread), plus homemade desserts, pies, cakes, puddings, or cookies.

For supper we ate leftovers, or cornbread and buttermilk, a southern favorite.

My closest neighbor, "Miss Susie" Anderson, often called in the morning. "What are you going to boil today?" she'd say. We thought we had to have something boiling in a pot for hours, field peas, pinto beans, collard greens, all with slices of salt pork called streak-of-lean. We didn't yet know about fats and cholesterol.

Refueling, we called it when Kirtley came in to eat. KW was now old enough to work on the farm in summer also. So during hay season I sometimes took meals to the field and we ate in the shade of trees bordering the field. Fried chicken, potato salad, homemade cake, and buckets of sweetened iced tea. Sweet tea is the southerner's standard nonalcoholic beverage.

Brother, Frances, and Sheldon Jr. (Buzzie) moved back to live on Brother's inheritance down the road from us, and it was good to have them nearby. Brother opened a law practice in Marion, added to his property and started a dairy, working in the dairy before and after full days in his office. Always fit and energetic, he'd say, if he found me in bed with a cold or headache, "Get up, Sister. Get out in the sunshine. Breathe the fresh air. You'll feel better."

Sketchy notes of the time show people coming for dinner, supper, to spend the day, the weekend. We didn't entertain in the usual sense, with parties or crowds, but we had a varied assortment of friends, a few close friends, and a steady social life.

I enjoyed it all. My creative needs were satisfied, I thought, with sewing, trying to make the house attractive, crimping piecrusts, finding antiques in junk shops. But something still seemed to be missing. It was like eating all that good food and feeling not quite full. Or maybe it was feeling *too* full. I'd learned so much, seen and felt so much, that I wanted somehow to save it, to share it.

After dinner each day, I was free for a while. At first I read: *War and Peace, Walden, The Sound and the Fury, Out of Africa, Moby Dick,* whales and all. I subscribed to the *New York Times Book Review* and tried to keep up with what was being published.

5

TRYING TO WRITE

BEFORE LONG, INSTEAD OF READING after dinner, I began trying to write and focused on the short story, a genre I considered my size. I'd been writing all along, dozens of weddings and funerals as favors for friends, and special events for local newspapers. Back in Auburn I'd begun numerous stories but hadn't known how to finish them.

And I'd been reading the great short story writers, Ernest Hemingway, Chekhov, Katherine Anne Porter, Katherine Mansfield, the short stories of Faulkner and Tolstoy. Flannery O'Conner hadn't yet come on the scene.

When KW entered first grade, I began writing most of the day. As soon as the schoolbus drove off in the morning, I hurried to the typewriter. Kirtley was already out on the place.

My stories didn't succeed because I hadn't yet learned the basic techniques of the craft: beginning, complication, climax, reversal, denouement, and ending. And I didn't understand the all-important meaning of theme.

In 1949 I sent a manuscript with pay to the Shipman Service, New York, one of many sources, sometimes spurious, always advertising help for would-be writers. I happened to receive one valuable reaction. "This particular manuscript is a difficult one because of its being a personal experience presented more as if it

Clothes shopping for Kirtley W., which he hated, in Selma.

were an article or portion of a novel rather than the story situation of a character."

In other words I was still, as back in Auburn, taking the route of amateurs and writing about myself disguised as protagonist or, at worst, heroine.

Years later after my book *Tongues of Flame* was published, and

I'd learned somewhat better, I wrote in answer to questions from a Gadsden, Alabama, High School English class:

> "None of the stories in *Tongues of Flame* are autobiographical, in the sense that they are about me or my life. Yet I have drawn freely from my own experience and that of everyone I've known, even casually. Facts, people, places, have been recycled like tin cans or newspapers.
>
> In fiction there is tacit understanding between writer and reader that the writer and his ego will step aside in order to communicate on a deeper, nonpersonal level. The deepest level, reached in great art, is universal.
>
> The characters in my stories are composites. They were suggested by aspects, physical or psychological, of real people, but I did not take the people bodily from life and put them in the stories. Each one had to be made up or made over to fit the needs of the fiction. The imagination works on this like a child at play, with whatever happens to be in his playroom."

When KW was seven, I was offered the job as editor of the *Marion Times-Standard*, Marion's weekly newspaper. Previously, while the editor was hospitalized for alcoholism, I'd worked as guest editor for several months at a time. I'd loved the shop, the excitement, the feedback, and of course the writing. I'd written not only news but editorials and features, everything except sports and ads. So the only limit was my strength and ability, and I'd tended to work all the time while things went rapidly downhill at home. When Kirtley brought KW by the office to see me in summer, he'd be wearing a sweater. In winter he'd be in shirtsleeves, and he seemed always to have a cold. Kirtley too looked unkempt and neglected. So when I was offered the job permanently, I didn't take it.

And soon there was Little League baseball. KW, left-handed by nature, showed exceptional promise as a pitcher. Kirtley had played baseball at Baylor University, his Alma Mater, so he was the at-home coach. They read books on technique and practiced, practiced, with Kirtley as catcher.

When Marion's Little League team played neighboring small towns, KW began pitching shutouts. I knew he shouldn't pitch until his pitching arm was sore. But the focus was on scoring during games, and KW pitched too long repeatedly. From the *Marion Times-Standard*, June 28, 1956:

> Kirtley Brown, who struck out 18 Greensboro batters in a seven inning game last week, turned in another stellar performance. He allowed only three hits and struck out 13 Greensboro batters to bring his strikeout total to 31 for his two games during the season.
>
> A large crowd attended the game which was played at Johnson Field.

So he "threw his arm away." By the time he was in high school he could no longer pitch and had to play left field. But he also played basketball in season, and became a lukewarm Boy Scout. Since he was still too young for a driver's license, I was his driver.

I kept no record of those years but I must have been writing all along, because in the fifties I was sending out stories and collecting rejections. One of the stories, never accepted, was about Little League baseball, titled "The Price of Glory." Personal experience presented as fiction, no doubt.

The book that I found most helpful at the time is still in print and still a favorite, *Writing in General and the Short Story in Particular*, by Rust Hills. Hills was for many years fiction editor of *Esquire*.

Kirtley W., left-handed Little
League pitcher.

Marion, like Auburn, was a college town, home of Judson College and Marion Military Institute. Like Auburn, the social life was active. My friends in town belonged to study clubs, garden clubs, bridge clubs, civic clubs, Daughters of the Revolution, the United Daughters of the Confederacy. When I didn't join a group, I was often asked, "What are you doing out there?"

"Trying to write," I'd say.

I'd get a puzzled look and change of subject.

In 1952 I enrolled in a creative writing class at the University of Alabama, Tuscaloosa, an hour and a half from our house. At first I drove up alone for two of the three weekly morning classes. But Kirtley didn't trust my driving, so wound up driving me, after he'd worked on the farm all day, to the one long night session. He spent my class-time in the university library, which he enjoyed.

But someone, usually Betty, had to stay with KW who had lessons and school the next day. And we all had to get up early the next morning, so the venture was doomed from the start.

But by listening to other would-be writers read aloud to the class, I began to grasp the meaning of theme. Years later, to winners of a citywide writing contest for high school students in Mobile, I tried to make it clearer: "The theme of a story is something a writer feels in the beginning, the conscious or unconscious thrust of what he has to say. It's the path the story takes, and the writer learns to *feel* when the story gets off the path."

I'd read that the theme of a story can sometimes be stated in a single sentence, but I'd never been able to find one. Years later, the theme of my story "It Wasn't All Dancing" became an example. The aging southern belle's life, with its alienated daughter, lost love, and no money, hadn't been all dancing, after all.

In 1954 I wrote Miss Mary E. Henry, Bureau of Correspondence Instruction, University of North Carolina, Chapel Hill.

Dear Miss Henry,

I need help in short story writing. I attended a seminar in fiction writing at the University of Alabama winter before last, but still have not been able to sell. Since I have a husband, child, and household it will be impossible to go to the University of Alabama again, even once a week as I did then. That winter nearly killed us all. . . .

For the past four years I have tried to write short stories. More accurately, I have written short stories and tried unsuccessfully to sell them. . . .

I have manuscripts on hand if one must be submitted.

So I was given as teacher a poet living in New England, Charles

Edward Eaton. His several books of poetry had blurbs by such notables as Louis Untermeyer, John Hall Wheelock, Witter Bynner, and Paul Green. The modus operandi was that I mail stories to him and he mail back criticism. It was he who told me to submit to the literary quarterlies, of which I'd never heard. He suggested quarterlies that he considered best, and I began to get acceptances.

The first acceptance was from the University of Kansas *City Review*, Kansas City, Missouri, May 27, 1955, a story titled "The Flesh, the Spirit, and Willie Mae."

I remember feeling deeply, interiorily, gratified. I'd connected with another human being in a distant place. It was what I'd hoped and tried to do.

Kirtley was a habitual reader, but not of fiction. He wanted me to succeed but didn't usually pay attention to what I was writing. He'd happened to put his mind on the plot for this story, however, and it was his idea to have the wife's husband bring home a TV instead of a washing machine. It was the twist that made the story work, so he was tickled to know that the story had been accepted.

KW was excited when he came home from school. I'm sure I called Lamar and Martha Holley in Birmingham. Dr. Howard Lamar Holley had grown up with me in the Hamburg community and had become a renowned rheumatologist at UAB. He would write *A History of Medicine in Alabama*, published in 1982. He and his wife, Martha, were both readers and had encouraged my efforts from the start.

But here at home we didn't drink a glass of celebratory wine or do anything special. Except in my own consciousness, the acceptance didn't dominate our day.

The story was not chosen as one of the twenty-one *Best American Short Stories, 1956*, edited by Martha Foley, but it was on her list titled "Distinctive Short Stories in American Magazines, 1955."

Also on that list was "By the People" by William Faulkner, published in *Mademoiselle*, and "You Can't Be Any Poorer Than Dead" by Flannery O'Conner, *New World Writing*, No. 8.

I don't know whether it was this time or another when I showed Kirtley some small recognition a story had received. "Don't tell anybody," I remember telling him. Since I was writing and hoping for publication, I don't know why I should have felt secretive about it. I realized, I suppose, that not many people would be interested, and that others simply wouldn't like what I'd written.

"The Gesture," another story from the University of Kansas *City Review*, soon appeared in a short-lived publication titled *Best Articles and Stories*. It brought my first piece of fan mail, from Tulsa, Oklahoma, in 1958. I had other stories in *Four Quarters*, La Salle College, Philadelphia, and *The Carolina Quarterly*, The University of North Carolina.

None of these stories are what I now consider good work. They were unfulfilled promises, and I hope they never again see the light of day. But I later considered a few worth rewriting. "The Flesh, The Spirit, and Willie Mae" became "The House That Asa Built," in the collection *It Wasn't All Dancing*.

I was keeping a journal, as writers are advised to do. I called mine work-books and filled them with whatever I thought might be of use as germs for stories, as description, the flora and fauna at different seasons, apt similes and metaphors, bits of dialog, or examples of transition (transitions are tricky for writers). Sometimes they were simply narrative fun.

1956. Story idea. Old preacher F, retired and visiting everybody sick. Somebody at the Bazaar, "Oh, that's the old man that runs everybody crazy at the hospital and nursing home."

As catching as a yawn.

Character. The magazine lady.

Telling of husband's incapacity, her struggle to make a living. Blood pressure over 200. Doctor said, You can't have anything good to eat any more. No coffee.

Nice wedding band, engagement ring, cameo in V of dress. Marks of onetime prosperity, gentility. Long, slender fingers, nice hands. Teetered when she walked. "I get a little dizzy sometimes."

Kirtley: "Last thing I need is more magazines. I ought to be trying to sell you something."

She. " Well, I couldn't buy a sack of candy. I'm broke as a haint."

K. "Sold cattle yesterday. Market off."

She. "Be thankful you've got something to sell. I've got nothing but somebody else's magazines and I can't sell them."

I told her she needed to find rich people.

She went up to Mr. L's and told him I said he was rich, could buy anything he wanted. Told him her tale of woe. He gave her $1.00.

Do a First Person Story

RB told me, "All you have to do to write is get off in a house by yourself and get lonesome."

The way a print begins to appear in developing fluid. First outline, then details.

The Amber Lamp. E.(household help) broke my amber lamp, one of a pair, prize possessions. She doesn't seem sorry. *Why?* Story would be why. End might be dream, the amber lamp in place and lit up, illuminating the reason.

Men in the locker plant in their bloody white aprons. Locker plant good setting for story. That deadly freezer part is dangerous. If anyone got shut up in there he'd be a goner.

Do story about NR, how I liked her till everyone said she was nutty. Eyes like someone who just waked up from sleep, fresh, vague.

Back to the magazine lady. I was mad at her for what she told Mr. L. But she was staggering under heavy load of trouble, needed help. Well, I helped her and the magazines have piled up unread for a solid year.

Southern names. Ravenel, Bragg Pitts, Val Taylor

Breck sent word to K to come to the mountain oyster supper and "blow the soot out of his flues."

So hot candles are reeling out of their holders.

(From the following I wrote a story, never finished or submitted)

I was hospitalized with bronchitis after a storm blew part of roof off our house. I was put in semi-private with another country woman, on other side of curtain.

At first my heart went out to her, poor, illiterate, neglected teeth, sun baked face. When she told me she had eleven living children and one dead, I was her slave.

But soon it was, "Will you git up and roll my bed up just a little?

"Hand me one of your magazines, hon, when you git through with it. I need something to look at."

"When your husband comes, tell him to bring us a newspaper. I want to see if that storm hit where my oldest daughter lives at."

"Go out there in the hall and tell one of them nurses to come git my bed pan. I got to pee."

She said she was chilly. I got up and turned off the air conditioner. Then she was hot and I had to turn it back on.

The first time I had a square meal, they brought hamburger steak, rice and gravy, iced tea, etc. It looked wonderful and I was starving.

Mrs. S. "Didn't that doctor say they was to give me a enema this morning?'

I took another bite, said nothing.

"My bowels hasn't moved since Wednesday morning."

I tried to think of something else.

"That doctor told them to give me a enema this morning. They don't do nothing right in this place."

I gave up eating. They gave her the enema.

When I have company she butts right into the conversation. Listens to every word. Quizzes me about the visitors after they go.

Comment on Sunday dinner. "Here's a piece of chicken big enough to kill a nigger."

Her visitors troop in, chewing gum and coughing, worse than I did when I came. I try to breathe lightly, hoping the germs wouldn't get to my bed. It soon came out she didn't want all those children, just too ignorant to know about contraceptives. Husband always off in beer joints.

Practical nurse came in to make beds.

Mrs. S. "I think I'll set up while you make it up. I wisht I'd brought my house slippers, but I was taken so sudden I never thought of nothing. Not even a comb."

Nurse. "You mean your hair hasn't been combed since you've been here?'

Mrs. S. (whiney voice) "No ma'am, it hasn't. I told my husband to bring a comb, but you know how men is."

I'd just put up my own comb, but said nothing.

Practical nurse. "I've got a little comb in my purse. I'll go get it."

When she brought it back, she gave me a dirty look going by.

Ending. Back at home, they'd cleaned everything up. Before I dropped off to sleep, I thought, I should have given her the comb.

Wind so strong the birds are like upstream swimmers.

Walking back home today, my shadow walked ahead of me, led the way.

EV told me about two sisters, widows, one in Mobile, one in Marion. They visit back and forth, want to live together, but neither wants to give up her house.

"My house has more room."

"But there are more doctors down here."

B and wife, visiting. His once beloved "Mama" now such a problem, he said, they had to move out of state. "She wouldn't leave us alone," he said.

His father had been a drunk. Mama had worked, kept family together, did without everything. In school B was always talking about what he was going to do for Mama when he got out on his own.

Me and Betty going to see Joanna, stopping for can of beer. . . (this became the story "Beyond New Forks").

In September 1956, I received a letter that brought, in time, not only a literary agent but lifelong friend. I'd read the review of a book by Victor Chapin, a conscientious objector during World War II. He'd done alternate service in a mental institution and had written a book, *The Hill*, about the experience. My college roommate was in such an institution so I ordered the book, read it, and was impressed by the quality of his writing. I wrote Victor Chapin and said so. This, in part, came in reply.

> *Dear Mrs. Brown:*
>
> *How good of you to write. I received your letter today and hasten to answer because it seems to me to have that extra something that encourages communication. . . . Funny, one gets strong impressions of people from these letters, and my impression of you was particularly strong. I felt immediately that you are a writer, a good one, I mean. Having worked for some time as a reader for a literary agent, I have become addicted to a kind of intuitive judgment of people and their talent. Glib, perhaps, that's the danger, but necessary in work of this kind.*

So, after letters back and forth, he recommended me to John Schaffner Associates, the agency that handled my work (that is, sent out my stories and collected rejections) until I stopped writing at the end of the fifties.

6

THE TWENTY-FIVE-YEAR SILENCE

I REMEMBER THE DAY I decided to put writing on hold. KW was now a teenager, living in the country with no brothers, sisters, or nearby companions. If he wanted to bring friends home, I found it hard to say, "You can't, I'm working." He understood what I was trying to do, wanted me to succeed, sympathized with my difficulties, and seldom asked.

This day, though, he had two boys from town out for the day. They were shooting basketball goals in the back yard. I was upstairs working on the end of a story where the words had to be right. The right words were out there like fish nibbling at my line, but they wouldn't bite so I couldn't reel them in. And it was time to start lunch.

So I went down and began banging pots and pans around in the kitchen. Writing had become obsessive and I resented any interruption. I no longer wanted to cook, clean up a room, feed anybody. I wanted to manipulate words into characters and situations, fresh similes, authentic dialog.

And I felt on the brink of being able to do it. I didn't think I'd ever be a Flannery O'Conner, but I thought I could be a quality writer, that I could tell what Katherine Mansfield once called "my own little grain of truth." It would take an all-out effort on my part, though, while Kirtley struggled with real-life problems on my behalf, and KW, whom I'd brought into the world, needed a mother, not a writer. Or so I thought at the time. To put writing aside for the present was a gut decision and a relief.

Meanwhile, changes on the farm and in the area had been taking place as definitely as the seasons. The transition from row crops to cattle had caused black people who'd lived on the place for years, if not all of their lives, to start leaving.

In 1955 Rosa Parks refused to give up her seat on a Montgomery bus. Strong tremors were felt in Hamburg, and the moving picked up speed. Soon only a blind man, Willie Morgan, called "Stone," and his wife, Claudia, called Claudie, were left on the place. Those who had raised me were dying out.

Mammy's second daughter, Betty Holmes, had washed and ironed our clothes until she retired.

Betty was a perfectionist. One day, passing a pair of pajamas she'd ironed and laid out on a table, Kirtley said, "Betty, those pajamas look so good I'll have to put on a tie when I wear them."

Now Betty lived with Nannie in Mammy's old house. Both had grown old. Betty had taken care of Nannie, bedridden with rheumatoid arthritis, until she, Betty, began to give out. So we took Nannie to a nursing home for black people in Mount Vernon, Alabama, but Nannie wasn't happy there. "They won't let me have but one dip of snuff a day," she told Betty.

So Betty, on her own, arranged to have Nannie brought home. One winter both were sick in bed with flu at the same time. I took down trays of food and medicine twice a day, and tried to clean up.

"Where'd you empty the slop jar at?" Betty asked one morning.

"Right back of the house," I said, and pointed.

She turned her face to the wall and groaned. "On my collards!"

After a week, I began to wear out. "Betty," I said, "I can look after one of you in bed, but I can't look after both. We'll have to take Nannie back to Mt. Vernon."

"Didn't nobody ast you to come down here," Betty said shortly.

Next morning when I went down, she was up with a pot of coffee brewing in the fireplace, the only source of heat they had except a wood stove in the other room. She didn't intend for Nannie to go back to Mt. Vernon where she wasn't happy. So Betty kept Nannie until Nannie died. Then Betty moved to Marion Junction to be near her blood kin.

When President Johnson made his "We shall overcome" speech in 1965, Kirtley and I listened with Brother and Frances at their house. Brother, a Reagan Republican, always owned the best television set in the neighborhood because of his interest in politics. He'd once run for probate judge and been defeated. We sat in his living room and listened in silence.

"Bloodshed," Brother said, when it was over. "There'll be bloodshed."

He was right. March 7, 1965, was Bloody Sunday in Selma, and we became the epicenter of the Civil Rights movement. All of our lives, black and white, were to change forever. To this day, with a population 30 percent white and 70 percent black, we remain on the cutting edge of ongoing changes, hard to understand by people elsewhere.

My story "A Meeting on the Road" deals with this change. The problem of race, into which I was born and have lived all my life, has been in my psyche, my heart, and my work from the beginning. Four of the eleven stories in *Tongues of Flame* are about race: "The Cure," "Fruit of the Season," "Let Him Live," and "Beyond New Forks." The title story of the collection *It Wasn't All Dancing* has a racial relationship as subject. "Swing Low," the memoir, deals with race from an earlier time.

After so many departures from the place, Ollie Lee Smith, an independent WWII veteran who lived nearby, came to help Kirtley and work on machinery. Will Naves and Robert Smith stayed to help feed and look after cows. During hay season Kirtley drove a truck to Marion each morning for pick-up help.

Those who wanted day-work gathered at a designated store to be picked up. Kirtley, Ollie, and KW drove the machines that mowed and baled the hay. Day workers were here to pick up the then-small (now large) bales, load then onto trucks, and store them in the barn and hay house. Riding past our house on the trucks, they stretched out on hay bales and sang freedom songs. They brought no lunch, so it was my job to collect canned goods, hoop cheese, sweet rolls, and soft drinks to feed them. Occasionally no workers at all were at the store.

And the pastures, once lush with crimson and white Dutch clovers, had lost vitality. They needed fertilizers we could ill afford. Cattle prices continued to fall so that we, with many other cattlemen, decided to sell our cows and look for new options.

We decided against a dispersal sale, with an auctioneer, big tent, barbecue, and country music. Over in a day, rain or shine. Our banker friend, Victor Atkins Sr., advised us to sell our herd of 598 gradually, as opportunities and buyers appeared.

I kept a haphazard calendar for 1967. We first sold yearlings, then cows and calves. And buyers began to appear almost daily.

"Time to go down and sit in the lobby." Kirtley said one morning, as we dressed to go downstairs after breakfast.

Luckily, soybean farmers from outside the area were looking for land to lease in the Black Belt. It was a godsend for us. We met with several prospects, agonized over a decision, and finally leased our land to partners from Arkansas, H. L. (Chick) Hill and Ray Trantham. Chick, a successful farmer and landowner in his own right, would stay in Arkansas. Ray, with his wife and two sons, would move to Hamburg.

Ray was a master farmer, bringing with him state-of-the-art equipment. Kirtley laughingly said one day that Ray could part your hair with a piece of his machinery.

Ray ate dinner with us January 1, 1968, and I cooked traditional southern good-luck food for the New Year, blackeyed peas with smoked hog jowl, collard greens, and cornbread.

So Ray and Chick, of Trantham-Hill Farms, farmed our land until Chick died and Ray retired because of heart problems. It was a relationship without problems or dissension for over thirty years. Ray became like a member of our family.

In the meantime KW had been at the University of Alabama School of Commerce, on his way to law school. I got my daily writing fix from letters to him, which he somehow kept. Mostly chit-chat and news of his friends, they also gave insights into our lives at the time.

"I've been helping Dad with his baby calf project, but it's too fraught with heartaches for me. They get sick and die too much. Also he doesn't keep his bottles clean enough, and I keep them so clean it takes hours and hours."

"When we got home last night (during a minor drought) we found 24 calves out in the church yard eating all that high grass. They weren't about to go back in that barren pasture, no matter how Dad hollered and waved his crocus sack. When they took a notion to move, they went loping across our nice lawn, making big holes with their feet in the damp ground, grabbing a bite or two of whatever shrub they went by. Then they headed straight for Miss Susie's lawn, and the first raindrops were falling. Dad got out the little truck, which didn't start too well after Will's (a helper's) wreck last weekend, and finally got below them, then ran and yelled and waved until they came back up toward the house where I was stationed, waving my raincoat like a bullfighter. We finally, in the rain, got them in that lot in front of the house. I wanted to go out and hit each individual one."

"Betty has gone. She moved down with Willie Fuller (her son). Two truck loads of stuff. It was a sad day, the end of an era. There has been a member of her family—first Mammy, then Nanny, then her—in that house ever since I was born, and before. Mammy came to work for my parents when they first came to Hamburg, when they lived in the top of the store. I cried and Betty cried, but time marches on. She couldn't stay down there alone."

"I'm getting on with Thoreau. I'm over to Solitude now. I read about Thoreau's life in the Brittanica. He was in love with Emerson's wife. . . .

"We wish you could be here today. We're going to the river to pick violets this afternoon and take a picnic supper for the Inges. (Part of our place is on the Cahaba River. Long-stemmed wild violets, deep purple and fragrant, grew along the edge of the woods.)

"Dad told me two days ago to send you his 'regards' and I forgot. Yesterday he asked if I did, and I had to fess up. So here they are— regards from your adoring father."

"Uncle Bob and Aunt Sara came to Selma on business and we had lunch with them. Uncle B was upset. They'd had car trouble with his Mercedes. It just stopped in the middle of the highway, with all the Chevrolets and trucks going on by, Aunt Sara said. She doesn't like that Mercedes. . . .

"Yesterday in Selma I bought a pecan tree for the front yard, which Dad and I set out in the afternoon. This morning I'm getting ready to bake a cake for my son, who will be home the day after tomorrow!"

"Since you're going to be around drinking from now on, there's something you may not know. The way fraternity boys drink can be dangerous. Alcohol is a powerful sedative, and it works on the brain, putting to sleep first one brain-center, then another. You can see the effects, loss of coordination, speech, equilibrium, etc., not in that order. I don't know the order. But enough alcohol will put to sleep the center which controls breathing and kill you dead as a hammer. . . . If anyone drinks this way and doesn't vomit before it all takes effect, it just plain stops breathing. When Bill Morgan and Jennie (my Judson roommate married a doctor who was the college physician) first went to Chapel Hill, he right away had a case like that, a fatality from overdrinking. It's just one of those bad things you have to know, like carbon monoxide in a parked car. So if you ever see one of the brothers getting like that, stop him. You may already know all this. I'm just so anxious to give you the benefit of everything I ever learned from all these years of being alive."

"I ordered a copy of *Ship of Fools*, Katherine Anne Porter's long awaited novel, as a present for Mr. Wiggins. I thought we should give him something as token of appreciation. . . . Everyone interested in American Literature will be dying to see what it's like, I'm sure. Granville Hicks in the *Saturday Review* says it's not a masterpiece, as everyone hoped; but Paul Pickrel in *Harper's* says it is. So that makes it even more interesting."

"I ordered all this good stuff to read and that's what I'm doing mostly. I'm about to finish Christopher Isherwood's new book *Down There on a Visit.* Then I have the new O. Henry Awards. Reading all this good stuff makes me a little itchy to write again."

"I had the Marion Drug mail you a good nylon toothbrush yesterday. It's soft enough that you can brush your gums when you brush your teeth, using those up and down strokes. Please use it."

"Did you know Dad is treasurer of the Cattlemen's Association this year?" (Kirtley W was treasurer of Phi Gamma Delta fraternity, 1962, I think. None of these letters were dated, other than Wednesday, Friday, etc. Stamping on the envelopes is often hard to read.)

"They are expecting a sit-in demonstration in Marion tomorrow. It's Martin Luther King's wife's hometown, you know. Mrs. Middlebrooks (café owner) told us they'd been told to let them come on in and not protest, then call the law." Oct. 5, 1962

"Feb. 20, 1962. We just saw Col. Glenn shot into space. It was a memorable moment. . . . I'm still in orbit too. Claudie's (blind man's wife) reaction. 'Well, I 'clare fore God, I'm glad it ain't me!'"

"I managed to make a dozen chicken salad sandwiches for the church supper. It went off very well, but not many people came. Dad was at his funniest on the way home, going on about the discussion during the Lenten study part. Someone got off on the Jews trying Eichman, and so forth. Dad said Coleman (priest) can't get blood out of turnips and shouldn't let us say anything, just look at the cross for a while and go on home. He said, 'All Sheldon and I did was sit there full of sandwiches, absolutely no intellectual activity in us at all.'"

"Uncle Bill came by yesterday. They're just back from Hot Springs, where he had good luck at the gaming tables, went night-clubbing, ate fine steaks, and heard Jane Morgan."

"I'm thankful to be sitting here writing as usual today. We almost had an accident going to Janie's last night. We went the back way and were batting along in the pouring rain when we hit the runners on an old bridge and Dad lost control of the car. I was taking a blueberry pie to Janie and didn't get scared because I was so intent on holding onto the pie—but it was like riding a bucking horse for a few minutes, or seconds. If the car hadn't come out of it, I guess we would have gone in the creek. Oh, well. It didn't happen, but dad said it was the closest to a bad accident he ever came. We came back by way of Greensboro."

"Dad has built an electric fence (one strand) around his oat patch, but he has one smart cow who knows how to get over, or under, it. He's out here now trying to un-learn or out-smart her."

7

MAJOR CHANGES

ON MAY 29, 1966, WE WENT to Tuscaloosa to see KW graduate from college. The next day we brought him home with a BS degree in commerce and a commission as second lieutenant in the U.S. Army. He'd taken ROTC since his last year of high school at Marion Military Institute. After three years at Perry County High School, we'd sent him to Marion Institute as a boarding student. We thought the change would begin to loosen home ties for him and for us, before he went off to college.

Two years later, January 1968, the year we sold the cows, he was graduated from the University of Alabama Law School with a Juris Doctor degree.

And our lives rushed forward. He came home, studied for and took the state bar exam. Not knowing whether he'd passed or not, he went to his first Army assignment at Ft. Gordon, Georgia. When the bar report came, we sent a telegram that said, "Hallelujah!"

Kirtley and I flew up to visit him at his second assignment, Ft. Lee, Virginia. It was the first five-day vacation we'd ever had, and we had a wonderful time.

On October 29, he called home.

"Mother," he said, "Are you standing up?

I said that I was.

"Maybe you better sit down," he said. "I have orders for Vietnam."

"I'm going to call Uncle Travis," I said. Travis was now a brigadier general.

"If you do," he said, "I'll never forgive you."

He wanted to go, was set on going. So I didn't call, wouldn't have anyway when the shock wore off.

Many people carry dates in their heads, birthdays of friends and relatives, special events. I don't have the gift (I've had to hunt up every date mentioned so far), but the years 1969 and 1970 are burned into my memory as with a cattle brand. All during KW's time in Vietnam, I bore up by telling myself that if I lived through that year, no other year in my life would be as hard. It was a prophetic fallacy.

He arrived at Tan San Nhut Airfield, Vietnam, January 6, 1969, soon after the famous Tet offensive. He'd been prepared for Military Intelligence at Ft. Lee and later Ft. Hollibird, Maryland, so he was sent with an Advisory Team of five Americans to the Mekong Delta. They were to advise and support three Vietnamese companies surrounded by Viet Cong. They lived in a small, hastily constructed wooden Team House protected by sandbags, and took turns staying awake to keep watch at night. An airplane flew in once a week with supplies, and they did their own cooking. Sometimes they went out on operations. Once they did a 30-mile march.

Ever since my confirmation, I'd been active in St. Wilfrid's Church, Marion. Now I was up there all the time, polishing brass and silver, setting up for Communion, arranging altar flowers, bringing home altar linens to wash and iron. Altar Guild members are "God's housekeepers," I'd read, so I held the primitive hope that this service would dispose the Almighty to protect our son.

And my daily letters began in earnest. KW wrote often too,

sometimes every day at first. Our RFD postman, George Hewston, blew his horn when he had mail from VN so we could rush out and get it. KW kept, and somehow managed, to bring my letters home.

18 Feb. "Evidently you've still had no mail from us, though I've been writing every day, including letters I mailed in Marion on Sundays. We're finding all the places on the big map (we had a large map of VN tacked to a wall in the breakfast room where we watched all possible newscasts). . . . I calculate by the ruler that you will be situated somewhere in the Mekong Delta. I read somewhere that the war will be won or lost in the Mekong Delta."

Kirtley wrote 2/14. "Dear Ace, Mama is polishing brass at the church and I'm going to Selma to get my suit altered. Am also paying our income tax today. . . . Wish I could be there in your place."

16 Feb. "Unc Bob and Aunt Sara called last night. They're getting a big map and following all the newscasts too. Your whole family will be fighting with you, if that's any comfort."

19 Feb. "I've thought of one thing in Vietnam I don't have to worry about. You can't imagine how glad I am that I thought of it. I don't have to worry about your being *cold*. You know how it always distressed me to think you might not have on a sweater or warm enough coat. It's a small thing, but a comfort."

28 Feb. "Dr. Weissinger (physician and close friend, retired army colonel, personal physician to Gen. Douglas McArthur, WWI) just called and said there was one thing he forgot to tell you about your weapon. He said he'd already told you not to hesitate to use it. If

you make a mistake, he said, it will be bad but you will be alive. The other thing that bothered him that you might not know, he said. Don't aim at the head, chest or legs. Aim at the belt. Right at the belly button, if possible. Anywhere else, except around the belt, they can kill you while they're dying. Dr. W. is anxious that I pass this on. So this is the second letter today."

1 March. "All the Fittses—Unk Sheldon and Aunt Frances, Buzz, Bev, and both children are going up to Illinois, leaving next Sunday. Buzz is going to a dairy school to learn to do artificial insemination, just for their own herd. The families are going for pleasure, since it's spring holidays. Aunt Frances is a Chicagoan, you know, she and all her family. I know they'll all enjoy it."

"The news sounds bad this morning . . . so please be extra vigilant. . . . As incomprehensible as it seems, you're in a war!"

"Last night Chet Huntley said there had been Communist attacks from 'one end of Vietnam to the other.' Now that we're in it, I don't think the commentators do a good job of covering the war. Those of us involved consider it the most important news in the world. Yet every night we must first listen to student uprisings, Sirhan Sirhan's trial, dead birds on the West Coast, etc. Finally they give us a little piece of news like that, accompanied by no map with dots. I think I'll write David Brinkley and tell him his son should be in the war. They merely mention peace talks, maybe once a week. But that's the tragedy of Vietnam. No one pays any attention until it really strikes home. Until then, it's just a bad, sad thing for other people, off somewhere. . . ."

22 March. "I want to take this opportunity, as they say, to thank you

a million times for your letters. You cannot imagine how much it means to us to get them. We will never be able to thank you enough for writing. You are getting us through the war, really." (Kirtley had mailed him, and he'd received, a small manual typewriter.)

March 25. "Mr. Pope (our Marion grocer) died yesterday and Miss Laurie (his wife) wanted me to 'write up' the funeral. So I went up yesterday afternoon to get material. Had a visit with the widow of Mr. Pope's late partner. She's a cute old lady all dressed up in a crepe dress and gold beads, and said she knew I'd do a good job and 'to put some love in it.' Dad will be a pallbearer.

I have the story ready, only waiting to check a couple of dates. Worked on it until 11 p.m. and got up at 5 A.M. I did 'put some love in it' and hope it shows. I put some love in this too, as you know."

March 29. "Take care of yourself. To us you're not just another solder. You're all that we have."

7 August. "We had promised Billy Crew to celebrate when he got his masters at Birmingham Southern. I called Miss Erin (his grandmother) to see when he'd be through. It's today, so I told her to tell him to come on down to supper tonight. . . . Dad had told Billy earlier that to celebrate he was going to get drunk and let Billy watch him (Billy had never touched a drop in his life). Dad told Billy this the last time he was here. Billy didn't laugh when Dad said it, but apparently laughed all the way home and told his folks. They all thought it was hilarious. I do too."

2 April. "Dad said our sweet postman, who blows the horn when he has a letter from you, came up for a visit Monday, a holiday because of Gen Eisenhower, and brought a doz. big brown eggs and a

pigeon. . . . I forgot to tell you that Dad is back in the pigeon business. Mrs. Kirkpatrick unloaded on him last week. She's a Selma lady, wife of an eye, ear, throat doctor. Has a lovely pigeon loft, very fancy."

April 11. "I know you will do your duty to the best of your ability, because that's your nature. I know you will even go above and beyond your duty. But, for our sake, try also to survive."

12 April. "We've been hearing that the VC have been shelling Long Vinh in the Delta, and then the commentator will say 'and 35 other towns and villages.' I'm so glad we're entangled in the store sale (we had to sell all contents and fixtures from the store before it was torn down) so that I'm forced to hold myself together and face people and put my mind on whatever comes up next. Then at night we're so physically exhausted we fall into these bottomless sleeps.

"I know you're calling on reserves of stamina and mental discipline you never knew you had. So are we."

16 April. "Last night I decided to make cookies for you from a recipe calling for applesauce. This, I thought, would keep them nice and moist for the two-three weeks it takes to reach you. But Miss Susie (neighbor) thought it over and decided that applesauce might cause the cookies to mold or sour. 'You don't want to make the child sick way over there,' she said.

"Life has become very simple. The only thing I want in the whole world is for you to get safely home. I know Dad feels the same way. No more goals, ambitions, or desires—only that one elemental wish."

20 April. "I sent you a clipping from the Wall Street Journal or Na-

tional Observer in which someone said the war in VN is histori-
cally already over. I thought later I shouldn't have sent that to you.
Besides, I don't know that I believe it. The news seems to ebb and
flow in that direction. For the past few days it has seemed that Ha-
noi simply will not agree to anything reasonable, but intends to
try to wear us down to win. Or fight on until the protestors and
public opinion force the issue. . . . The more I read the less I seem
to understand."

24 April. "We've had letters from you every day for several days
so the mail plane must be coming out more often. Today you've
been at Phuec Long three weeks, seven to go. I'm not surprised
you forget what day it is, but I don't, I assure you. I check them off
thankfully every night.
    "How's the Sargent's cooking?"

2 May. "We went to sleep last night listening to Ray's tractors working across the RR. They're planting soybeans on the day and night
shifts, before another rain. The place looks good.
    "Yesterday we mailed you two boxes of food. In the big box is a
small canned ham, which you all must eat up at one meal since you
probably have no refrigeration, and other canned stuff, like those
party frankfurters and party salami I got before Mr. Pope's store
closed. . . . I tried to send enough for all of you."

5 May. "One little item I've meant to tell you for days. Did you know
the average weight of a Vietnamese soldier is 104 pounds? That's 11
pounds less than *I* weigh."

3 June. "We're sure you're in Saigon by now, and hope you've had
a good hot bath and a few other niceties lacking at Phouc Long.

We also hope you have a pleasant week there and get to see the Staff Judge Advocate. I have little hope about legal work for you—especially after the two intelligence schools. I hope it will come to pass, nevertheless."

7 June. "Dad coughed up a little blood the other day and went to see Dr. DeRamus yesterday afternoon. (He'd been a heavy smoker for years, had been told to quit after bouts of bronchitis and pleurisy.) Dr. D. said he'd like to run some tests in the hospital and told Dad to come in this morning. . . . I imagine they've started the tests by now. They brought in cartons for sputum samples for each day through Sunday. Dad hasn't seemed to feel bad. He'd had a bad cough just after the store sale, but went up for medicine and it cleared up."

9 June. "According to Stone Hodo (hospital laboratory technician and Judson classmate) there is nothing wrong with dad. She thinks he had a low-grade pneumonia recently, hence the chest business. However Dr. D is giving him a thorough physical, heart, kidneys, stomach, gall bladder, the works. Dad feels good and is having a lot of company and attention."

14 June. "I brought Dad home yesterday afternoon. Dr. D said he found nothing wrong at all. He thought he'd simply had bronchitis in his chest."

June 29. "I find that I'll have two weddings to write this fall. Also, it seems I may be teaching Sunday school if Bob Miller (our priest, later Bishop of Alabama) can get someone else to take over the altar. They're in desperate need of a SS teacher. He thinks Evelyn Wilsford will look after the altar if I take the little children. I mean *little*. Pre-school."

26 July. "This morning I read over all your letters about the legal possibilities. I went back to when you said that, starting in August, every defendant in the Army would be entitled to a lawyer (not captain or major) to defend him. (New law just passed.) I do believe, that even if the job with Cpt. Barrett falls through, some other legal opportunity will come up for you."

5 August. "Dad is trying to paint the front porch, and has gone to town for supplies. I am, as always, doing battle with disorder and dirt in the house. On the side, I'm studying the S.S. material and wishing I hadn't said I'd do it, though I'm sure I'll be glad when I get involved with the cute little children. The other day I picked up the phone (party line) and Miss Susie was saying hello to one of her grandchildren, or great-grands, 'How are you, little devil?' she said."

The legal opportunity did come up. At the request of Capt. Lionel Barrett, a Nashville lawyer in JAG, KW was moved from the Delta to Can Tho, which may have saved his life. He'd also been promoted to first lieutenant.

"It's a beautiful day here at home. Sunny but unusually cool. Everything is a lush green from all the rains we've been having, and the Mimosa trees are in full bloom. At night the scent is strong on the air. We also noticed the first fireflies of the season Sunday night when we cooked out in the back yard. Ray's tractors are running in the distance, the birds are singing in every tree, it seems, and this does seem a good place to live. I suppose only the middle-aged love home in this way, if they're fortunate enough to have a home with roots that go back a way. Your Vitex tree should start to bloom soon though it is our latest bloomer."

30 June. "We had a visit from your cousin Margery Cunningham (Travis' daughter, married to Capt. Lee Cunningham). Five little children 10, 8, 6, 4, 2 brought up under 2nd generation Army discipline on both sides. They don't go through the house grabbing things, though they're interested in everything, and very, very bright. One asked Dad how old he was. Dad said he couldn't bring himself to tell him 66, so he wrote down the year he was born and they figured it out."

2 September. "Your phone call made Labor Day a Red Letter Day. I was so nervous that when I put down the phone I saw it was completely wet where my hand had perspired. But you sounded wonderful, and we know now that the reassignment has gone through, that you will be going to Can Tho in two weeks, that the trial went well and your client walked out a free man. . . . I woke up and got up at 5:00 this morning, just to enjoy thinking about it. Before I got the coffee-water hot, Dad came creeping into the kitchen too.

"We're under the impression that Can Tho will be safer, our main concern. Also more comfortable as to quarters, food, surroundings. And then you'll be getting experience and using your profession. What more could we ask? You're old enough to know that, as James Branch Cabell said, 'Wherever a man lives, there will be a thorn bush near his door.'"

9 September. "This is the day of Household Reckoning. When I'm working on a project like getting ready for that S.S. class, Dad goes on vacation, besides being retired. I know everything from back porch to bathroom is going to pot, but I don't *see* it in detail until there's a breather. Then I see it all, in detail, and I'm furious and frustrated. I begin sweeping under tables and chests, mopping up dust that has lain there peacefully for ten days, gathering up maga-

zines and newspapers that are strewn over every surface. I can never understand that Dad will sit contentedly in the midst of all this dirt and disorder, when he has nothing to do but what he pleases. I've now scrubbed the back porch sink, which was filthy, and really cleaned up the breakfast room, which seems to get more cluttered than anywhere else, so I decided to let off steam to you, halfway around the world, trying to fight a war!

"Well, I didn't decide to tell you. I just did. You will know that home is the same as ever. . . . Meanwhile, I have to get out wedding stories and pictures to the Selma Times-Journal, the Montgomery Advertiser, and the Birmingham News."

Sept. 16. "Big news today. Col. Robinson called last night and offered Dad a job (Marion Military Institute) in Col. Woodfin's office, helping get out publicity and working with the annual and newspaper. Dad did this kind of thing in Auburn before you were born. He's going up to talk to Col. Robinson in the morning, and thinks he will give it a whirl. Col R. said it could be part or full time, and they'll talk about it in the A.M.

"It was a compliment to Dad that Col R offered him the job. We were quite excited last night, and couldn't get to sleep until midnight.

If Dad goes to work at M.I., I'll lose my household help—so I must get the most out of him today. We haven't vacuumed the house, for one reason and another, in two weeks. I must get him to clean up the sleeping porch before his reassignment!"

26 Sept. "Four grand letters from you yesterday. . . . You and Cpt. Barrett are certainly busy. I do feel for the soldier whose pistol went off and shot the bar girl. Of course such a thing would never have happened had he been at home. In the first place, he wouldn't have

had the pistol in a bar. He's probably sick with the horror of being involved in it. He could be a war casualty because of it. He could be just a bum, but he could also be a pretty good boy, and a victim. It seems to me it would be a great satisfaction to be a lawyer, and have the privilege and ability to help people out of messes like that.

"I'm still working on my clothes for tonight and Sunday afternoon. Over the years I've felt guilty that I didn't, back in Auburn, "help" Dad as I might have by going to all the functions, willingly and interestedly, like some wives did. So now it seems I have another chance. I'm going to dress up and go and enjoy this stuff."

10 October. "The 'Sherry Delight' cupcakes (white fruitcake cupcakes) I mailed yesterday didn't taste as good as the previous ones. But the main ingredient in them is your mother's love, so whether they taste good or not, I hope they bring a whiff of the kitchen at home."

Oct. 6. "My SS class was wild today. I had a grand session prepared, I thought, on the Lost Sheep Parable. We were to play a lost sheep game, with the shepherd blindfolded, finding lost sheep by their 'baas' of distress. Then we made little sheep out of white pipe cleaners and cotton balls. Plus the usual ritual, songs, etc. But I couldn't seem to hold or unify their attention. Debbie (Judson girl helper) was in there trying too, but we simply didn't bring it off too well today. Debbie is going home next weekend and won't be there. Dad (who was also there to help) says he's going to have a sick headache. They were too much for him today. But not me. I still *love* those children."

13 October. "Consciously or unconsciously now, I feel my attention centering on one thing, your homecoming. Please take care of

yourself. Wear that .45! The military seems to expect a new winter offensive."

10 Dec. "Your birthday (Dec. 24) cake was upside down and thrown into a corner before it ever left Marion! The man in the P.O. grabbed the box and put the stamps on upside-down, so it will travel on its brandy glaze. . . I hope it will be waiting when you get back from R and R (Australia).

"When I went to mail your cake, Dad helped me get the box outside the tin wrapped. Then we ate supper in the Mess Hall at M.I. with Major Boner.

"Your Xmas card from Saigon came yesterday and I let Dad take it up to keep on his desk until school is out. Wasn't that generous of me?"

14 Dec. "Yesterday when I read your letter about the Bronze Star, I immediately went in to call Dad. I couldn't get him, but just at that time he called me. I told him that they were going to give you the Bronze Star and started crying and couldn't say another word. He had to wait a while and call me back before he could hear what you'd written."

At this point I began preparing for KW's return. The Second Coming, his Uncle Bob called it. Kirtley loved his job at Marion Institute, left early in the morning, and was gone until suppertime. So I found help for the heavy housework and swept down walls, washed windows, waxed floors and furniture, polished silver, dusted books. Toward the end, our current priest, Father Bob Miller (later Bishop of Alabama), relieved me of the Sunday school, so I put on finishing touches and bought champagne and flowers.

We met KW at the Montgomery airport, 2:52 A.M., Jan. 24,

1970. We'd gone far ahead of time to circumvent any eventuality such as car trouble, flat tire, or accident. Once there, we huddled together on a hard seat in the empty waiting room and dozed for two or more hours. Kirtley had been fighting a cold for a week or more, but in my frenzy of preparation I hadn't paid attention. I'd baked a ham, a chocolate layer cake, and loaves of bread. I'd made homemade mayonnaise and cooked everything KW had liked.

It was cold when he got off the plane in a short-sleeved fatigue uniform, but I'd taken a jacket. He was thin and subdued, but apparently all right. We asked if he wanted to eat breakfast in Montgomery or go on home. He said go home, so we came straight back. He drove, as I remember.

I hurried to the kitchen to start the first-meal celebration, but Kirtley said he was sorry, he'd have to go up to bed. He'd looked forward to this moment for months, so I knew he was sick. KW ate hurriedly, and we too went to bed.

But Kirtley got up feeling better and we had a happy Sunday. Monday morning he went to work, and the next afternoon to Dr. Arthur Wilkerson, another Marion physician (we used both). Dr. Wilkerson prescribed cough medicine, which seemed to help.

But the following Monday morning I had a call from Dr. Wilkerson's office. They'd made an appointment for Kirtley with a Birmingham surgeon, the nurse said. So we drove up the next day to the New Baptist Medical Center, where Kirtley was scheduled for a lung biopsy the next morning.

After the operation, the surgeon told KW and me, as we stood up in a waiting room full of strangers, that Kirtley had inoperable lung cancer, that it was already in his lymph system. With treatment, he could possibly live two years, the surgeon said.

So we went home and began trips to Birmingham for cytoxen.

After the third bottle, Kirtley went back to work at M.I. and the cobalt treatments began.

All of our friends and family came. Travis came from San Francisco. Bob came from Opelika, where he'd moved his law practice from Auburn. There was an outpouring of help and concern as can only come from a small town and community.

Cobalt treatments continued until the end of March and, except for trips to Birmingham, Kirtley went to work as usual. Lamar and Martha Holley kept us going with medical and moral support and advice.

And KW began looking for a job. He'd sent his Army pay home for Kirtley to bank, so he could now buy the MG he'd wanted. He found a job with Hugh Caffey, an established lawyer in Brewton, and moved to Brewton but came home on weekends.

Kirtley began to be in pain that we couldn't control at home. He'd spend a few days in the hospital, then a few days back at home. Finally one night Brother drove both of us to the hospital to stay. We had a large room at the end of a hall in the Perry County Hospital, a small-town hospital where everyone knew us and felt for Kirtley. On one side of the large room was a Naugahyde couch where I could sleep when Kirtley slept, be up when he was awake. The hospital sent me three meals a day.

We were there for three months. Travis' wife, Margery, came from San Francisco and stayed for a while at our house in the country. Kirtley's sister, Irene Brown Weaver, a teacher in Texas, came when her school was out. She came to the hospital at mid-morning each day, had lunch with me, then stayed with Kirtley while I went home to wash clothes, pay bills, check on the house and yard. And feed the multiplying pigeons.

And Kirtley suffered. It was if a torturer, off somewhere, kept planning what to do to him next. When he was pain-free from drugs, he pulled himself together as from a trip to hell. He didn't complain, didn't talk about his condition, kept his sense of humor. And one day he said to me, "I never wanted you to go through anything like this."

On our thirty-first wedding anniversary a friend, Millie Davis, made a cake with candles. Irene brought presents and we had a party in the room. Kirtley was able to enter in, then had a terrible night.

On July 24, 1970, five months after his diagnosis, on Friday, as if to make it convenient for KW to be there, he died.

We had a simple graveside service in St. Wilfrid's cemetery, just behind the church, the next afternoon. His friend, Neil Davis, Editor and Publisher of the *Lee County Bulletin*, Auburn, wrote the following obituary.

"They buried Kirtley Brown in the little Episcopal Churchyard cemetery at Marion last Saturday. He had suffered the ravages of lung cancer since the first of the year. We did not learn of his death in time to get to the funeral Saturday, but we drove over Sunday to see his wife, Mary T. and then to his grave. Kirtley was a long-time friend. Our friendship dated back to the early 30's when this editor was a 'Plainsman' reporter and he was news officer of the college here.

Kirtley served Auburn with distinction first as editor and later both in that capacity and as student affairs director. It was only natural that he would join the college staff after graduate work at Yale University in 1927. His family had deep roots in Auburn. His father, Dr. J. V. Brown, was one of the college's early football stars who later became director of buildings and grounds and alumni secretary. He has two brothers who are Auburn alumni (one of them is Roberts H. Brown, Opelika attorney). The Brown family bought the antebellum house known today as Noble Hall and painstakingly and appreciatively restored it.

Longtime residents of Auburn remember Kirtley best for his warm human qualities. He was a gifted, intelligent man possessed of such modesty that he sold himself short. He was self-depreciating but in no pious, offensive way. Rather Kirtley's view of himself was flavored by a sense of humor that made for laughing with him, never at him. He was sensitive of the feelings of others and so was kind and compassionate. His values were good; he held to them in times of stress as well as ease. He was generous with his time in serving the general welfare and with his worldly goods in sharing with others. And long before it became fashionable to talk about the needs of the poor and disadvantaged, Kirtley quietly put himself on their side. He instinctively was for the underdog.

When in 1946 he and Mary T and their little son Kirtley Ward (now a fine young lawyer in Brewton and carbon copy of his father) moved away to farm those beautiful acres at Hamburg in Perry County, our contact with him became all too infrequent. Nevertheless, we both knew about the fortunes of the other, and our friendship was rooted in shared experiences and convictions so that it never diminished. Last fall he wrote from Marion Institute that he had come full circle—back to handling a publicity job for M.I.— and at age 67 it was clear that he was tickled at himself and over prospects there. It is too bad that cancer felled him a few months later. He had so much to offer that fine institution.

They don't come along very often—men of the strong character and sweet spirit of Kirtley Brown. We will miss him, as will many others in this college community who had known him as friend and colleague."

8

ALONE

So, at fifty-three I WAS A WIDOW. People said, "What are you going to do? You can't stay out there by yourself."

I didn't know what I was going to do, but I couldn't imagine going anywhere else to do it. Except for the seven years in Auburn, I'd lived in the same place, most of it in the same house, all of my life.

Irene, long divorced, was still with me. She lived in Texas simply to be near her two married daughters. So she was glad to stay, would have stayed on.

But I wanted to face my situation as it was, and would be. On my first day alone, three weeks later, I wrote in my week-at-a-glance calendar, "defrosted fridge, wrote a few thank-you's, cleaned downstairs, burned trash."

Unlike the widow in my story "A New Life," who couldn't cry, I cried all the time. Alone in the house at night, I cried out loud like a wounded animal. Out in public, a word of sympathy would undo me.

I no longer went to church. Watching Kirtley suffer such pain and indignities had shattered my faith. I felt alone not only at home but in an indifferent universe.

But someone had to take up where Kirtley left off. He'd looked after the place, balanced the farm and personal checkbooks, paid bills and taxes. I was gently notified by our accountant that our income tax was overdue. John Furniss, of Furniss and Vaughan, Selma, who'd been Daddy's accountant as well as ours, came out to the house to help me get it ready.

I ordered a refresher course, *Working with Numbers*, and studied while learning to take over the business of house and farm. I made trips to banks, the USDA Farm Service Center, the Social Security office, Furniss and Vaughan. And to the cemetery, where I had a Brown headstone installed.

At night I was sometimes afraid, so I had opaque shades put on the windows, deadlocks and chains on the doors. A neighbor, J. C. Thompson, an electrician, installed the siren from an old fire truck in the attic of the house, with a switch beside my bed. Our dog, McArthur, a large liver-spotted pointer, was a good watchdog.

My immediate goal was to keep the home fires burning for KW, who came home most weekends.

In a notebook dated Aug. 25, 1971, I wrote:

> K has been dead one year, one month, plus one day today. It wasn't a bad day as days go since he died, but I am so lonely the main thing I remember is someone passing me on the way to town and waving up ahead, an exaggerated gesture full of good wishes. I could only see his right arm moving, and the back of his head, but it gave me some kind of a lift.

Soon after, in appreciation of his maybe having saved KW's life, I invited Cpt. Lionel Barret, now back in Nashville from Vietnam, with his wife and young son, for the weekend. Bob came to join us for a meal of standing rib roast, and KW showed the Barrets the area, including Moundville State Park with its preserved Indian mounds and exhibits.

Later in September I wrote,

> For most of this first year, I have simply grieved, not so much
> for myself as for Kirtley—if he was all right, if he still *was*. And I
> wanted him back, had recurring dreams about his walking in the
> door, always the back door, as if sneaking him in against all reason.
> . . . Now I seem to be in a new stage that began coming on, I think,
> with the fall. I seem to be concerned not so much with him and
> his future as with me and mine. I'm alive, for whatever reason, and
> must make something of it.

In November, Bob died, also of lung cancer. Like Kirtley, he'd
been a heavy smoker. In the past, he'd smoked Picayunes.

I still had trouble sleeping and if I slept, woke up in the middle
of the night. One early morning I got up and watched the sun
rise from my bedroom window. In one of my old work books I
wrote:

> First it was flamboyant, rose and grey, layered and shifting, low
> in the East. The rose got rosier. Then it all seemed to dissipate and
> fade out, upward and outward as if it was all over, except for a small
> red area down low which appeared to be coming to a head. The red
> deepened, began to enlarge and, very slowly, to rise. It took almost
> an hour, give or take a few minutes.

> Another day. "A kind of workaday sunrise, mostly hidden by low,
> lumpy clouds the color of factory smoke. Now and then through a
> hole in the smoke, you could see a heavenly blue and pink. The ac-
> tion seemed fairly high in the sky most of the time, and then the
> rapid dissipation of color followed by an all-over lightening. And
> finally down low, a crescent of not so much color as radiance. Not
> red, orange, yellow, but a molten combination."

So watching the sun rise took the curse off early waking. "It's there every day," I wrote.

I made a list of what I considered no-no's and pitfalls for widows.

Trying to make the marriage sound perfect.

Always talking about the lost one. "He used to say . . . . He used to tell me . . . . *Especially,* he wouldn't let me."

Making people feel guilty.

Hanging on to grief.

Going to scenes that bring back the loss.

Complaining to people. Listen to their complaints but keep your own to yourself. You're not looking for pity, but . . . what?

By 1972 I'd thought of trying to write again, and of Victor Chapin, with whom I'd lost contact. He was now working full time at the Schaffner Agency, where he was later to become vice president. So I wrote, and sent him a story.

"Good writing," he responded, "but not a story. Try again."

In return he sent me a book manuscript of his own to criticize. Victor had been an actor before he was a writer. He was a graduate of the Carnegie Tech Drama School, had appeared on Broadway, and had played supporting roles to the likes of Orsen Welles and Luise Rainer. Now he wanted to be a writer, was a quality writer, but his work didn't sell and make money. My stories didn't sell at all, so we were a comfort and support to each other.

He invited me to New York for Thanksgiving, 1972. My friend Janie Allen, an older widow, farmer and antique dealer, who lived in nearby Newbern, went with me.

Janie had been my and Kirtley's longtime friend while he was living. Now she was a role model in my grief. She'd been widowed with a nursing baby and three small children, plus a farm in debt. She'd raised and educated her children, paid off the debt, bought more land, and started a successful antique business. When Kirtley died she began taking me with her on buying trips for antiques, across the state and to nearby states.

For our New York trip she carried on the plane, all the way up, a large bucket of fall flowers from her large country yard. It endeared her to the New Yorkers, if not to fellow travelers who had to steer clear of our bucket.

We didn't stay with Victor and his partner, Jack Van Bibber, on West Street, but ate most of our meals there since Jack was a gourmet cook, author of the book *Fast Feasts*. We saw an Arthur Miller play, an opera, a musical, and went to a loft where we were offered a joint. We visited museums, bookstores, and walked around the Village, shopped at Saks Fifth Avenue, and visited the show room of Jeremy Wren, who designed Mrs. Nixon's inaugural gown. We had a wonderful time.

Back home, Brother had asked KW to be his law partner. So KW came home to live with me, and Brother hung out a new shingle, Fitts and Brown.

And KW had met a girl, Susannah Metz of Birmingham, a gifted teacher, working at Blount High School, Mobile. He brought her home for a visit.

He'd also been to a meeting of the American Bar Association in England, where he was invited to stay at the home of an English solicitor, Anthony J. Holland (later to become Sir Anthony), and his wife, Kay. KW wanted to reciprocate, so I invited the Hollands for a visit and included Susannah.

Soon after, in 1973, the following announcement appeared in *The Birmingham News:*

> Mr. and Mrs. Wilbur Hinkle Metz announce the engagement of his daughter Susannah Lynn to Kirtley Ward Brown, son of Mrs. Charles Kirtley Brown and the late Mr. Brown of Hamburg, Ala.
>
> Miss Metz is the daughter of the late Mrs. Helen Cole Metz. Her grandparents are the late Mr. and Mrs. George Landess Cole of Marion, Ind., and the late Mr. and Mrs. Edgar Henry Metz of Indianapolis, Ind.
>
> Mr. Brown is the grandson of the late Mr. and Mrs. Thomas Ira Ward of Hamburg, and the late Dr. and Mrs. James Vandiver Brown of Auburn.
>
> The bride elect was presented at the Poinsettia Debutante Ball, of which she was charter president for 1968–69. She was graduated from Christian College in Columbia, Mo., and received her BS degree at Auburn University. She is employed in Mobile County.
>
> The prospective bridegroom was graduated from the University of Alabama, where his social fraternity was Phi Gamma Delta, and received his JD degree at the University Law School. He served in the office of the Army judge advocate general in Vietnam and is a member of the American and Alabama Bar associations.
>
> The wedding will be on Aug. 18 at St. Luke's Episcopal Church.

There were parties in Birmingham, Mobile, Marion, and even Hamburg, where Brother's wife and Buzzie's wife had open house for Susannah. The wedding was traditional and beautiful. Travis came from San Francisco to stand in for Kirtley.

The newlyweds rented an apartment in an older house in Marion. Kirtley went back to work at Fitts and Brown and Susannah began a teaching job in Selma.

And four days after the wedding, I went to work as secretary to the Guidance Counselor at Marion Military Institute. I was now fifty-six.

I hadn't typed for speed and accuracy since WWII, and I'd never cut a stencil. In addition to counseling, Col. John Moore was the official Marion Institute tester, giving a barrage of IQ and other tests to cadets throughout the year. One of my duties was to type all of the names and test scores into columns. For a while I had to take butisol, a sedative no longer used, to be able to do it.

But I loved the cadets. My desk was in a corner of Col. Moore's small office, so I couldn't help seeing the boys and hearing their problems. I began inviting them out to my house to play with the dog, play their guitars, eat cookies (no longer homemade but sliced and baked from refrigerated rolls). Years later one of the boys, Clint Weekley, whose grandmother had made and sent him wonderful cookies, talked about how he liked coming out here and eating "those old cookies." Chuck May, who couldn't stand confinement and the military regimen, was about to leave school until he began coming out to hunt on the place.

For me, it was better than medicine. Cadets rode out to my house on bicycles, sometimes walked the six miles. They left messages in my mailbox, notes on my door. My phone was always ringing. They brought me up to date on music, movies, their own ideas. Though I was still essentially lonely, I didn't feel alone as before.

And I came to know two young intellectuals with literary aspirations. Eugene (Chappy) LeVert, who lived in Marion, was a student at Birmingham Southern. Stephen Zeigler, just graduated from Wake Forest and on his way to graduate school, had moved to Marion with his widowed mother. They had me read *The Kandy-Kolored Tangerine Flake Streamline Baby*, *The Doors of Perception*, and Jack Kerouac's *On the Road*. Steve taught me that Bob Dylan is a poet. He understood William Blake, taught Blake as a teacher's assistant in graduate school, and introduced me to William Butler Yeats.

The three of us listened to Bebop jazz: John Coltrane, Charlie Parker, Thelonius Monk, Billie Holliday. Jazz was my favorite music, perhaps from hearing black people sing and play harmonicas on the store porch as a child. The same haunting pathos was in Bebop and earlier jazz. I don't understand modern jazz.

And I began to tire of typing and cutting stencils. There was no other future for a woman at M.I. at the time (today a woman is Dean). So after a year and a half I resigned, and my interest turned like a weathervane to the literary. Steve, especially, with his passion for literature and writing, was an inspiration.

In my week-at-a-glance calendar, I began to write "started short story" and "working on story."

One day when I went to town, someone asked, "Are you still out there trying to write?"

The farm, leased, was doing better than it had when we ran it. So I thought I could afford a three-week tour of Europe. It was a valuable bird's-eye view but strenuous, and I came home with swollen feet and hands, diagnosed as possible rheumatoid arthritis.

I'd been overall healthy since Kirtley died, except for frequent and recurrent urinary tract infections. The new arthritis, treated with bed rest, aspirin, and Motrin, went into remission after a while. Later diagnosed as osteo, not rheumatoid, arthritis, it has been with me ever since.

I learned about, and began going to, literary conferences at the University of Alabama and Alabama College, now The University of Montevallo. At a Faulkner Symposium, I heard Faulkner's biographer, Joseph Blotner. At a Hemingway conference, I met Mary Hemingway and heard Alfred Kazin. Ms. Hemingway came late to one crowded session and simply sat down on the floor. After a startled second, chairs seemed to fly up to seat her. A Shakespeare Symposium featured a performance of *Pericles*.

And I was reading James Joyce and Joyce criticism, Flannery O'Conner and O'Conner criticism, studying the short story form and trying to catch up on learning in general. KW and I took a course at Judson for a semester, Great Ideas of the Western World. It met once a week with Dr. Jonathan Lindsay, later at Baylor, as teacher. We were the only students in the class, so we learned as much as we could handle.

Transcendental meditation found its way to Marion and I became a meditator, twenty minutes twice a day. In time, I went to a three-day intensive weekend in Atlanta, learned to do yoga exercises, and watched nightly large-screen lectures by the Maharishi. But I soon tired of the Maharishi. Rather than bliss out with him, I'd go on suffering with Jesus. My faith had come back, more or less. I was like the disciple who, when Jesus' followers were falling away at one point, said, "To whom else would we go?"

And I overdid the exercises, to find after coming home that I'd made a hairline crack in a vertebra. It took a week or two in the hospital, plus more weeks of recovery at home.

I still think meditation is good for a writer. It's a conduit to the subconscious, that treasure trove of assistance. But it has to be done regularly, and it takes time. I continued to meditate for two years, until I began to write every day. Then I gave it up for walking, a time-health consideration. I don't know of anyone who meditates today. It passed like a fad, which it's not.

9

BACK TO WRITING

To commit myself wholly to writing fiction, now that it was possible, was chancy, I knew. I was aware of the odds against success, and I knew my limitations. I didn't know enough, didn't have enough broad information to do the kind of work I most admired. I hadn't traveled or lived in New York or hobnobbed with writers. My life had been too circumscribed, and I'd kept myself too safe. I'd driven my little truck off the road many times but managed to get back on before disaster. So all that I knew was a little of the hearth and of the heart.

But I went to a series of lectures at Montevallo by Joseph Campbell, the mythologist. He said that to fulfill his destiny, a person should follow his bliss. Writing was my bliss and I was sixty-three years old, so it was now or never.

I'd written a story, not a very good story, "Last of the Species," about a young girl who kept her virginity in a first-love situation, and had sent it to Victor. About the same time Lamar and Martha had given me a potted amaryllis bulb for Christmas. I'd watched it grow and bloom with such fascination that I wrote, with apparent ease, a story, "The Amaryllis." I'd sent it to Victor as well.

In February 1978, Victor called to say he'd sold "The Amaryllis" to *McCall's* for $1200.

For a later written interview, I answered two questions about the story, "What is the significance of the three buds on the amaryllis plant, and was there some reason for using an amaryllis rather than some other bulb?" I wrote:

The story began with a bulb someone gave me for Christmas. I was fascinated by its growth and wanted everyone to come and see the bloom. The story grew from that. First came the judge, a made-up judge, who had to be what is called in the writing trade a sympathetic character, a character with whom the reader can identify. Minor characters appeared like actors trying out for parts in a play. This is all fun, exciting, like play. The hard part begins with making it all real, true to life, and with finding the words, the exact right words, to hold it together reading after reading. I had no conscious reason for putting three buds on the plant. A great part of fiction comes from the subconscious, which could have been suggesting the Holy Trinity, but not to my knowledge. I used the amaryllis bulb simply because it is so fast-growing and produces such spectacular blooms.

Later in the year Victor sold "Last of the Species" to *The U.S. Catholic* for $250.

After the story in *McCall's*, I met Crawford Gillis, a Selma artist near my age. Besides being a gifted painter, he was a scholar who knew literature, art, and classical music. He became my reader-critic, source of information, walking companion, and best friend until he died in 2002. He introduced me to his friends in Selma, Carol and Sam Sommers, Elizabeth and Wallace Buchanan, and Jerry Siegel, owner of the Siegel Art Gallery, and to others in Selma and Montgomery who cared about literature and who supported my efforts. Previously I'd known only a handful of people who were interested in my efforts to write.

I once misplaced all of my stories and couldn't find them, In one of my work-books, I wrote that Crawford said, "You have to find them. That's the whole record of a misspent life!"

I don't think he meant to say it, or if he really meant it if he did. But it gave me pause. I found the stories, of course, and never mentioned the comment.

We came to know a rising young photographer and outside-painter, Jerry Siegel, cousin of the older Jerry, born and raised in Selma but with a studio in Atlanta. We were excited about his work and loved his visits. He'd spread his work out on my break-fast room table and all over the room, for Crawford's criticism and my admiration. Later he became my photographer for all publicity purposes. He has the beautiful name, never used, of Jerome Emile Siegel.

I still had a church job, the Canterbury Club, a Sunday night sup-per meeting for Judson girls and Marion Institute cadets. I'd had the job for six years and loved the students. One, Bobbie Maude Weekly, who became a chemical engineer, now Bobbie Meacham, married mother of two, has been one of my closest friends to this day.

But I gave it up, gave up everything except my family and the people who came for impromptu visits, scraped-together meals, or to exchange news and problems. I'd become attached to many people, and could never bring myself to say, "Don't come. I'm working."

So I began to live a half-and-half life, getting up at 4:00 or 4:30 in the morning, working for several hours, then doing everything I'd done before. In my little week-at-a-glance calendars, the days were few when I wrote, "Worked all day. Walked with Martha." Martha was Ralph's wife. They lived just around the corner, and we liked to walk with my dog, or dogs, to Green Liberty Church and back each afternoon, two miles.

In 1980 Leonard Michaels came to the University of Alabama, Birmingham, as writer in residence. He was scheduled to teach a five-week creative writing class to nonstudents.

I'd read his two collections, *Going Places* and *I Would Have Saved Them If I Could*, and knew that he was hot on the literary scene. I'd been attracted to his brilliant, unique prose style.

By then I'd written "Goodbye, Cliff," "The Cure," "Festival Day" (which later became "Disturber of the Peace"), "The Black Dog," and "Fruit of the Season." So I submitted stories and was accepted into the class.

Leonard, called Lenny, had a profound effect on my progress. He liked my work and took me under his influential wing. He told me to tell more by telling less. "In the modern world," he said, "people don't have time for character development in the old way. Read Isaac Babel," he said. "Write like me."

He called the editor of a quarterly where one of my stories languished, recommended other quarterlies such as *Threepenny Review* and *Grand Street*. It was he who finally said I had enough stories for a book, when the idea hadn't occurred to me. He talked to the publisher, Seymour Lawrence, on my behalf long before my manuscript was submitted.

I've never known how to express my gratitude to Lenny, except with gifts at the time, and now it's too late. I lost touch with him when he moved part-time to Italy. But he and his then-wife, the poet Brenda Hillman, and their daughter, Louisa, will always have a special place in my heart. While in Birmingham they came down to visit one day. Lenny said he wanted to do something "real," so I cooked a country midday dinner. We went to tea at the home of my friend Carol Sommers in Selma, and from there to a junk shop. He was collecting antique tools and hoped to find one. He died in 2003.

Stories were now pushing to the surface like seeds from my psyche. I could hardly wait to get up in the quiet dark mornings, hurry down for toast and coffee, get back into bed face not washed, teeth not brushed, and set to work.

I began each day by editing in longhand all that I'd typed the day before. Starting with the first sentence, I went over each word, hoping to make the sentence simpler, clearer, more beautiful, I hoped. Then on to the next sentence, next paragraph. I added to the narrative in longhand, typed what I'd added in the afternoon, and was satisfied with as little as one new paragraph in a day.

And in my head I was working all the time, scribbling thoughts on scraps of paper, grocery lists, unpaid bills. When I woke up at night, I'd turn on a light and reach for pencil and paper.

Typing and retyping on a manual typewriter, then physically cutting and pasting, were endless. I wrote few sentences that didn't undergo changes. While in school I'd considered rules of grammar boring and unnecessary, not realizing they were meant to clarify meaning. If I'd known such things as that the adverb should go near the verb, it would have saved considerable rewriting.

I looked on any sentence that stood up as first written as a gift from a Higher Power, though I was never sure that Higher Power approved following my bliss with needs all around me. This had to do with my religion, though I seldom went to church, since Sunday was the best work day of the week. No mail, ringing telephone, or visitors. All of our priests seemed to understand so I felt a minimum of guilt. I was like the storied juggler, juggling before the Blessed Virgin as a gift.

Above all, I didn't want to be what I thought of as a "fictioneer." I wanted my characters to be, do, and say what they would do and say in real life. I wanted to tell the fictional truth.

Years later in a two-minute speech written, but never read, for the Hillsdale Award by the Fellowship of Southern Writers (time ran out for all acceptance remarks), I wrote:

> I never expected to be here. The body of my work is so small and limited in scope that it never occurred to me that it would be noticed, much less commended, by a society of writers I've known and admired from afar.
>
> Nevertheless, it has been my *aspiration* to write a short story so good and so true that a reader anywhere could understand, and even care about, the fictional populace of the troubled and impoverished Black Belt of Alabama. Not only that, but I aspired to take the story across the boundary from good writing to art.
>
> I haven't written the story. They all fall short, even after my utmost effort. Not one comes close to "Noon Wine," "Powerhouse," or "Everything That Rises Must Converge."
>
> But this award is a powerful incentive. I plan to go home, simplify my life, and try again.

In time I moved to a Smith Corona word processor, and later to an iMac computer bought with grant money from the Alabama State Council on the Arts.

The nineteen eighties were filled with exciting ups and heartbreaking downs. The greatest ups of the time, and of my lifetime, were the births of my granddaughters, Mary Hays Brown in 1982 and Helen Ward Brown eleven months later. My eighties calendars are filled with "kept babies," "to see babies." They were a bliss that surpassed writing. And since they lived only six miles down the road, I was able to be with them as much as their lives allowed, though never enough for me. The grandmother name they gave me is "Gaga."

On the down side, Ralph died at home of an unexpected heart

attack. Martha called me to come. When I opened the door I could hear his groans. She couldn't leave him in agony so I rushed to call an ambulance. Shaken and unprepared, I called 911. The number they gave was also unprepared. When an ambulance was finally dispatched, the driver couldn't find the house. Help came too late.

Meanwhile, probably with a prod from Lenny, *Prairie Schooner*, the University of Nebraska, had accepted "Goodbye, Cliff." "The Barbecue" was accepted by *Threepenny Review*, Berkeley, California, and "The Cure" by *Ascent*, Urbana, Illinois. And Victor called to say he'd sold "Disturber of the Peace" to *Grand Street*, New York, for $500.

Victor and Jack came for Christmas '81. They'd traveled widely, usually abroad, but this was their first trip to the Deep South. We had a quiet, close-to-home visit. Jack, with minimal help from me, cooked Christmas dinner for the family.

I was working steadily now, trying to write while looking after the house, yard, and farm. The house had to be painted, farm and personal checkbooks balanced, income taxes prepared and paid. I had to cook, eat, and clean up the kitchen.

With Chick and Ray, I had what was called an Active Participation in the lease. I paid a percentage of the farm expenses and received an equal percentage of the profits. All of it took time. By now I'd come to think of everything besides writing as a Practicality, a chore and intrusion.

Still, I was sending stories to Victor. In 1983 he complained of being unable to sell submissions, not only mine but everyone else's. He wrote that his blood pressure was high, he didn't feel well and was depressed. So I attempted to write a purely commercial story, one with romantic love and a satisfying ending. He submitted "The Evergreen That Lost Its Leaves" and it, too, was rejected.

A few nights later, Jack called to say that Victor had died of a sudden heart attack.

KW and I flew up for his memorial service. This time we stayed with Jack on West Street so as to be of help. All of Victor's close relatives had died except his aged father, unable to come up from Florida. Jack was estranged from all of his kin, so Kirtley and I stood in for the families. Jack made black silk armbands for us to wear to the service, and we sat alone with him on the front row. The service was moving and fitting, with a large attendance.

The next year I had an even closer loss, Brother. Years before, he'd survived colon cancer, but couldn't recover from what began as a virulent case of shingles. It paralyzed one arm, caused constant pain, and finally affected his kidneys. After being on dialysis for several months, he chose not to continue. In the hospital he refused all medicine and procedures, and died with a football game in progress on the TV in his room.

Brother had always been a beautiful loser. Partly, I think, from sportsmanship learned on the athletic field and partly from an innate generosity of spirit. It was the way he chose to lose his life.

While in New York for Victor's memorial service, I'd gone by the Schafner Agency. John Schaffner, the president, had died earlier and I didn't think the agency would continue. So I began sending out stories on my own, with no luck.

Victor's assistant returned the letters I'd written during the last years of his life. Victor had taken them from their envelopes and put them flat into folders, so none are dated other than Sunday morning or Friday night. Here are excerpts from a random few:

"Our goals are different, in a way. You want to make a lot of money, and I want to write one really good, first rate, short story, or short something. If I live long enough, I really hope to do it. What a struggle, though. I looked at my calendar this morning and saw that I'd been working on 'The Black Dog' for six weeks, and it's still not quite right."

"After we talked yesterday I realized you had somebody on another phone, maybe two somebodies. I should have been more brief. I guess all your writers picture you sitting there just waiting for their problems."

"I just hope the story (unspecified) is good. God knows I worked on it long and hard enough. It had become a way of life, almost. Get up, work on the story, do a few necessities, go to bed. After a night of sleep, there's the moment of truth when you see what's not right from the day before. You try to fix it all the next day. A whole day on a paragraph. Then to bed, and start over with a new moment of truth in the morning."

"The truth is, nobody can save anyone else. (Jack was drinking heavily.) You have to save yourself, and first you have to want to try."

"The story (unspecified) has taken a turn for the better. Once the theme finally revealed itself (there were so many possibilities, rejection, guilt, etc.) it began to take the right shape and get itself together."

"I'm down to about three sentences on the story. If you look for a word or sentence long enough, it will finally present itself."

"All this frustration (Practicalities, visitors) has me in a state of tension so that I can't sleep at night, or digest food. But I plan to stop it this very day. Last night I took a dalmain (sleeping pill) that knocked me out from 10 till 7:30. Now I've taken the phone off the hook and will, in effect, be away from home today."

"The weekend was awful for me. X came with his wife and baby. I couldn't say no. I was bone tired from trying to get that story in the mail. The last thing in the world I needed, wanted, maybe, was to buckle down to having company. They got here at 2 a.m. Saturday morning. . . . Oh, I love them and all that—but it was just hard. Sometimes I think you can't be a writer and be human at the same time. If you do good work, you have to put it first absolutely . . . . Those kids drove 9 hours to get here, and 9 hours back. And the truth was I didn't want them to come and was glad when they left. That depresses me no end."

"I read your prologue at lunchtime. You'll have to do that over. It's overdone. But there's good stuff in there too, like 'unseeing points.' It's the writing that's not so good. You write too fast, like Della cleans up. You have quality material here and getting it across won't be easy. But if you don't do it right, you might as well not do it."

"I should have realized the (book) rejection depressed you, and I should have found out about your blood pressure (I'd gone to N.Y. with a group from Montgomery, to see a large Picasso show). I get so many rejections they no longer bother me much, but then I don't make the investment you do. A novel is like a dozen stories. No comparison. Also I've had a few successes, enough to keep me going, and all that encouragement from Lenny."

On June 1, 1984, I wrote Amanda Urban of the International

Creative Management.

> *Dear Ms. Urban:*
>
> *My agent, Victor Chapin of John Schaffner Associates, died last year. I found your name in Literary Agents, by Poets and Writers, Inc. I'm writing because you are quoted as saying you become personally attached to your writers, two of whom are Raymond Carver and Bobbie Ann Mason. So if I could choose a new agent, I would choose you.*
>
> *First I must tell you that I write only short stories. I'm in love with the form and obsessed with the craft. I don't think I could write anything else if I tried. Also I'm neither young nor prolific. In fact, I'm a grandmother. On the positive side, I do work very hard, full-time, and hope to go on for years. When I say I work hard, what I mean is that my life's blood goes in it.*
>
> *One of my stories will be in Best American Short Stories, 1984, guest-edited by John Updike. I also have one on the distinctive list for 1983. They've been published in McCall's, Grand Street, Ascent, U.S. Catholic, Prairie Schooner, and The Threepenny Review. I have a collection of ten stories that I hope someone will publish. Victor had sent it out only twice, to Farrar, Straus and Giroux and Knopf. The enclosed came yesterday. (?)*
>
> *Unless your list is completely full, I'm hoping you will let me send my latest story, fifteen pages, to see if you're interested. In any case, you have my thanks and good wishes.*

I hadn't known that Ms. Urban, called "Binky" by her friends and clients, was the best, most sought-after agent in New York. But she took me on and became a friend as dear as Victor. I've made hardly enough money for the agency to pay for her phone calls and postage, but she gives me attention and support as if I were one of her stars.

She asked first to see not the latest story, but all of the stories. So I began doggedly going over each one from beginning to end, then sending them up to Jack, who was a first-rate typist. It took so long she wrote to ask about the holdup.

Jack delivered the collection in May '85, almost a year later. Binky read and sent them out in June. Because of her cachet as an agent, probably, she soon had a nibble, then an offer, a $6500 advance from John Herman of Widenfield and Nicholson of England, which had bought Grove Press. A week later she had a $10,000 offer from Seymour Lawrence, who was then at Dutton, and finally $13,000 each from John Herman and Seymour Lawrence. So I had a choice and called Lenny. He said take whoever would get the book out first. It was Seymour Lawrence, called Sam.

I've always been proud to be one of Sam's writers. An article in *M* magazine, March, 1988, described him:

> The polished, 62-year-old publisher is anything but an egotist or a publicity-hungry media creature. The print he craves is, specifically, his name in concert with any of the authors of "quality fiction" he's been publishing for three decades, first at the Atlantic Monthly Press, then the Delacorte Press, and now E. P. Dutton in New York.
>
> Lawrence operates that rarity in publishing—an independent imprint, a kind of private literary kingdom within the larger terrain of a publishing house.

In early 1986, less than a year later, I received a copyedited manuscript of *Tongues of Flame* from Dutton. The next month brought galley proofs, and on April 3 a bound copy of the book.

I'd been working on a new story, "Let Him Live," when the first ten stories were accepted, and had finished it in time to be included. So there were eleven instead of ten stories in the collection. I'd sent in the title "Beyond New Forks" but Sam thought it hard to remember and not evocative. He preferred *Tongues of Flame*, which was fine with me.

He wrote, May 20:

> The months leading up to publication are often the most agonizing for a writer, even writers who've had 9 or 10 books published. The waiting period can be painful and full of self-doubt. But you'll come through with flying colors. Your work has appeared in the finest literary magazines in this country and we can't all be wrong.
>
> Finished books will be ready in a week or ten days and Camille will send you copies.

I wrote, "It's good to know I'm not the only one whose spirits are fragile in face of what seems public exposure. I think that up to now I've felt that not many people read the quarterlies, so I haven't actually been brought to trial. Now it's as if the whole world will know—the curious, those of different taste, and worst of all, the ones who will *know*."

Sam wrote, "The advance sale for *Tongues of Flame* is beyond my expectations. We have over 3000 advance orders and it's still three weeks from publication. Most first collections of stories advance 1000–1500 copies. I'm very pleased."

The excitement began first in Alabama. There were newspaper and magazine articles, interviews, letters and phone calls. At a signing at Capitol Book and News, Montgomery, the owners, Cheryl and Thomas Upchurch, said that I signed as many books as Bear Bryant. The Marion and Selma libraries had signings. I began to get phone calls and letters, many from other states.

Sam wrote, "More good news. Pocket Books has made a floor bid of $15,000 for the paperback rights to *Tongues of Flame*. The original offer of $10,000 from Obelisk, Dutton's trade paperback line, was their maximum offer and Obelisk graciously stepped aside."

Reviews were generally good. The *New York Times* review, Aug. 24, 1986, was not a rave, but favorable. The reviewer said, "This isn't the Old South of tangled prose and gothic characters. This is the South where everybody is expected to behave himself, where people know who they are, and where good family recipes are handed down. Brown writes like a woman offering warm home-made bread."

And the book was listed on the Times Editors Choice list for the next two weeks.

But Jonathan Yardley in the *Washington Post* was damning. The bold headlines of his long thumbs-down review said, "Stories Short on Subtlety, Collection Marred by Transparent Themes."

He went on, "A handful of its 11 stories are interesting, but most are the work of a writer who has a great deal to learn about narrative and who has yet to find her own voice; her sincerity is evident, but so too is her artlessness."

Artlessness. That hurt.

But Sam wrote, "You're doing just fine and you have nothing to worry about. There are bound to be a few negative reviews, there always are, but I think there will be universal acclaim and I don't mean Birmingham and Montgomery.

The second printing should be in soon. This is an exhilarating and heady time. Enjoy it to the hilt. But be wary. I remember Katherine Anne (Porter) telling me after *Ship of Fools* was published, 'Angel, nothing fails like success.'"

And for the *Birmingham News,* Chappy wrote:

> There are many mansions in Southern writing: Faulkner's broken columned memorials to pride and misbegotten honor, O'Conner's severe clapboards threatened with unearthly fire, and Welty's subdued bungalows with their warm corners and cool, dark halls—to name only the most familiar, old establishment addresses. With her first collection *Tongues of Flame,* just published, story writer MWB has hung out her plaque. It serves notice of a quiet, craftsmanly attention to studied harmonies of scale, an art of understatement enlivened by a sly sense of ornament.

Sam not only worked tirelessly for his writers and kept up with them through letters personally typed on what I imagined to be an old Olivetti typewriter, but went to visit them. He and Joan Williams, his companion of several years, spent two days and a night with me in May 1986, just before *Tongues* came out. Joan had been Faulkner's enamorata in her youth. A Mississippi native, she'd met Faulkner as a college student. He'd sponsored the publication of her first book, *The Morning and the Evening.* She and Sam were en route to see Thomas McGuane, one of Sam's best-known writers in Fairhope, Eugene Walter in Mobile, and on to a booksellers convention in New Orleans.

With Thomas McGuane, Lemuria Book Store, Jackson, Mississippi, 1986. He was signing his book *To Skin a Cat*, and I was signing *Tongues of Flame*.

In early December Sam took Thomas McGuane, whose collection of short stories, *To Skin a Cat,* he'd just published, and me with *Tongues,* to signings at Lemuria Books in Jackson, Mississippi, and Square Books, Oxford.

I loved Tom McGuane and bonded forever with John Evans, owner of Lemuria. In Oxford, we had lunch at the home of Barry Hannah, another of Sam's writers whose wild, wonderful work I love, then visited Faulkner's home, Rowen Oaks.

I brought home oak leaves from Faulkner's grave and pressed them in heavy books. Later I couldn't remember in which books I'd pressed them, so it was always a surprise to open a book and find one.

Back home, there were "Practicalities." A new well had to be dug and a new pump installed for the house. I had to have cataract surgeries. There were trips to the Farm Security office, the bank, records to keep.

And I received my first award, the Alabama Library Association Award for Fiction, 1987, in Huntsville. I hadn't yet learned to prepare any words of acceptance and, too nervous to think, made a poor appearance.

Later there was a wonderful book signing at the Selma Dallas County Library, and the next Sunday afternoon a memorable autograph tea in the Greensboro, Alabama, Library. The women of Greensboro entertain like ladies of the Old South. They decorate with flowers from their own yards, large, stunning arrangements in beautiful containers. They make refreshments from old recipes laced with modern savvy. They use good linens and silver. What they do is uniquely southern and elegant. It's a privilege to be their guest.

I was relieved that friends, neighbors, and readers in the area seemed to like my book. If it had been reviled, like Thomas Wolfe's *Look Homeward Angel* in his hometown of Asheville, N.C., I wonder if I would have continued to write.

10

MY FIFTEEN MINUTES

TWO DAYS AFTER THE GREENSBORO TEA, Sam called to say that *Tongues* had won the PEN/Hemingway award. I called at once to tell Binky, KW, and Crawford. Binky said, "You didn't! Well, God-damn!" KW had a client and couldn't get away, but Crawford came out to be amazed with me.

The next day my calendar said, "Worked in a.m. Crawford and Jack (Jack Bush, close friend and supporter, our parish priest at the time) here in afternoon. Made scones."

Susannah had a lovely dinner the following Sunday, which was Easter.

Attention revved up, and I saw the way professionals do their jobs. First a reporter, Peggy Brawley, came from *People Magazine*. She arrived on time, when most people get lost on country roads to my house. We had lunch. She asked the questions she'd pre-pared, and was gone.

Then a photographer, Will McIntyre of North Carolina, came to take pictures for Peggy's article. He flew to Montgomery, rented a car, found the way to county road 45, then 12, and arrived at eight a.m. He carried equipment in the car and the trunk of the car, in every pocket of his jacket and cargo pants. He shot me in-side and outside the house, walking down the road with my dog, Boone, in a soybean field, and on my front steps with Kirtley, Susannah, Mary Hays, Helen, and two kittens. In Marion he shot me at Breck's where I liked to eat, looking in an empty store window, and in the cemetery where I'll be buried. Finally we ate at a beer and barbecue place, The Shack, and he left at 10:30 that night, fast friends to this day.

KW flew with me to New York for the award. We were met in a stretch limo provided by Jack Van Bibber, far gone in wine.

Binky took me to lunch and visit at the Algonquin. Sam and Joan took KW and me to the awards reception at 5:30, at Goethe House. I'd asked someone at PEN what to wear, and he said dress up. So I was overdressed in a black cocktail dress, when most peo-

With the family on my front porch. Kirtley and Susannah; Helen, blonde hair; Mary Hays, dark hair; blonde and black kittens. Photo by Will McIntyre, for article in *People* magazine.

ple came in casual clothes on the way home from work. This time, though, I'd written a speech and I read it. The date was May 27, 1987. I was sixty-nine years old.

When my publisher, Seymour Lawrence, called to tell me our book had won the PEN/Hemingway award, I thought of a Hemingway story I'd reread recently, "The Undefeated."

It's about Manuel, an over-the-hill bullfighter. Manuel wouldn't quit bullfighting. When the story opens, he's just out of the hospital but trying to find another fight from Retana.

"Why don't you get a job and go to work?" Retana says.

"I don't want to work," Manuel says. "I am a bullfighter."

Retana finally gives him a night fight, as a substitute, dangerous business at low pay. Manuel looks up Zurito, a picador he can trust.

"What do you keep on doing it for?" Zorito wants to know. "Why don't you cut off your coleta? You're pretty near as old as I am."

"I got to do it," Manuel says. "I got to stick with it."

Zorito agrees to pic for him, on the condition that if things don't go well the next night, Manuel will quit. "Will you do that?" Zorito says. "I'll cut your coleta myself."

"Sure," Manuel says.

So the fight takes place. Manuel has to try five times before he's able to kill the bull. Twice he's knocked down and the bull is on top of him. Each time he's back up, trying to kill the bull. His sword is bent. His face is bleeding. Retana's man hands him a new sword and says, "Wipe off your face."

The crowd threw cushions. An empty champagne bottle hit him on the foot.

In the next to last attempt Manuel felt the horn go into his side before the bull tossed him clear. He got up coughing, feeling 'broken and gone.'

"Go to the infirmary, Man," someone says.

"Get to hell away from me," says Manuel.

When he tries again, though, he felt the sword go in all the way. Right up to the guard. The blood was hot on his knuckles. The bull went down.

On the operating table, Manuel thinks, "To hell with this operating table. He'd been on plenty of operating tables before. He was not going to die. There would be a priest if he was going to die."

When he hears Zurito say something and hold up the scissors, Manuel sits up in protest and someone has to hold him down.

"I won't do it," Zurito said. "I was joking."

Hemingway writes, "The doctor's assistant put the cone over Manuel's face and he inhaled deeply."

Writers are like bullfighters in a way, always trying to get the sword in all the way, right up to the guard. Each new work, like each new bull, presents difficulties expected and unexpected, and requires desperate effort, at least from me, to be finished off.

Hemingway's life fell apart but his stories hold up, which brings up the old question of what is more important, the life or the work.

In any case, this story was an inspiration to me. Because he's a bullfighter, Manuel keeps on fighting bulls, against all the odds. He continues to try, to hope, and above all, not to let them cut off his pigtail!

Thank you for the honor you have done my work in memory of a great American writer, who once described himself as "Someone who gets up at first light and works hard at writing most of the days of his life."

Other awards were to be given, but on the far side of the crowded room someone fell to the floor by the cocktail table, and everything stopped. No one seemed to know if the person had had too much to drink, a heart attack, or worse. But he didn't get up and word flew 'round that an ambulance had been called. So we simply waited in place. The ambulance took a long, long time to come. When the fallen man was finally carried out on a stretcher, the event was simply over.

Sam and Joan took KW and me to dinner at Elaine's. Then they took me to their elegant house in Connecticut, while KW stayed in the city. The next afternoon Sam and Joan took me in Sam's Jaguar, driven by his chauffeur, Roy, to meet KW at Laguardia.

KW and I were back in Alabama by midnight and for me, as for Cinderella, the ball was over.

There were few worked-and-walked days for a while. I began to get letters and phone calls. Most of the mail was from Alabama and surrounding southern states, but there were letters from California, New Jersey, Illinois, all over. One was from a bartender in Albany, New York. He wrote that he liked my book.

> I thought I would drop you a line and tell you, since authors don't get the same feedback as actors or musical artists whose audiences are right there in front of them.

I tried to answer for a while. And I did readings in Demopolis, at Shelton State College, Tuscaloosa, (the Shelton State Readers Theatre did a presentation of "Tongues of Flame,") and at Georgia State University, Atlanta. I flew to Abraham Baldwin Agricultural College, Tifton, Georgia, and did readings at Livingston and Troy Universities, and at the Fine Arts Museum of the South, Mobile, with Eugene Walter.

Judson gave me an honorary Doctor of Literature degree, at the same time it gave an honorary Doctor of Letters to Barbara Bush, who'd flown down to be commencement speaker.

I didn't do all this with ease. I worried about, and spent time on clothes, shoes, accessories. I practiced what I was to read, or wrote and then practiced what I was to say. If someone was to pick me up, I cleaned up the whole house in case he or she needed to use that upstairs bathroom. And I always dreaded the moment when I would stand up before an audience.

I'd never been able to speak in public, not even with notes or note cards. Now I was called upon to stand up and read the stories I'd written before rooms full of people. Even with the story in front of me, it was always an ordeal. My hands shook and my heart raced.

Finally in Auburn at a statewide Read Alabama Conference, the kickoff meeting for a project to have Alabama authors studied in libraries across the state, I learned at last to read without dread.

My reading was scheduled for after lunch, with two writers ahead of me in the morning. One morning-writer read in a monotone. The second writer's plot was involved and hard to follow. My mind wandered. Around me, people began coughing and shifting about in their seats. I kept looking at my watch.

I couldn't eat lunch for wondering what I could do not to bore the afternoon audience. And that became my goal, not to bore the audience.

So I began to read slowly and distinctly, letting the story unfold at an easily understandable pace. For the first time I forgot myself and concentrated on the story and the listeners. The auditorium fell silent. I could feel the listening like an embrace. Afterwards, I understood why actors act and singers sing.

The experience took away my fear of reading, since I knew that it was at least possible to read well. But it was no help for speaking off the cuff or without a script. So from then on, whatever I've had to say in public, however brief, I've written in advance. Strangely,

I've never had trouble answering questions from the audience following a reading. Maybe I've felt that by then we were friends.

The Auburn meeting was memorable for other reasons. I heard a complimentary paper about my work read by Dr. Philip D. Beidler, of the University of Alabama. I could hardly believe he was reading about me. I met the beloved Jay Lamar who, with Leah Rawls, had originated the Read Alabama program. And in the audience was Dorothy Flynt who liked the reading, went home and told her husband. Dr. Wayne Flynt was the Hollifield professor of southern history at Auburn. Everyone knew him as the author of *Poor but Proud*, as a sought-after speaker, and for his many PhD graduate students teaching across the state. Dartie and he became supporters of my work, and the kind of friends for whom I don't have to get ready before a visit. In fact, they always brought the food we ate.

One morning in 1989 I answered the phone to hear amazing news. My story "The Cure" had been selected for inclusion in a Soviet-American anthology, *The Human Experience*. The caller was Janet Riley, Executive Secretary of the Quaker US/USSR Committee, Pennsylvania. She said that *The Human Experience* would be published simultaneously in English by Knopf, and in Russian by a leading Moscow publishing house.

She went on to say that the forty poets and short story writers included in the book, both Russian and American, were invited to a four-day conference in Washington, D.C., May 1–5, expenses to be paid by the Quaker Committee. And, even more astonishing, that the American writers had been invited by the Soviet Writers' Union to a reciprocal meeting in Russia the following year, 1990.

She hesitated, then asked if I was black or white. My story "The Cure" is about an old black woman and an old white doctor. I was pleased that she couldn't detect my race in the fiction.

This was the time of the Soviet Union, Gorbachev, glasnost, and perestroika. In a follow-up letter Janet wrote, "The intimacy of literature, with its capacity to represent the full range of human thought and feeling, is especially appropriate for launching this journey of exploration."

Norman Cousins, with a translator, was moderator for the all-day sessions held at the Friends Meeting House on Florida Avenue in Washington. We were treated to a reception at the Soviet Embassy and a poetry reading/book signing at the Library of Congress, but were also allowed considerable time on our own with the Russians.

With them we crossed the language barrier with gestures, improvised sign language, and spontaneous hugs. When they understood a compliment, they patted themselves above the heart. A translator was often there to help.

The entire meeting was a love fest. The Russians were fine writers, though none has been published here, that I know of, except the novelist Tatyana Tolstoya and the poet Yevtushenko.

Of the American writers present, the poet Sharon Olds was our eloquent spokesperson. There was also Stanley Kunitz, C. K. Williams, Charles Baxter, Henry Taylor, and Garrison Keillor, among others. I sat beside Garrison Keillor one whole day and we said not a word to each other, but when he spoke to the group and was translated, the Russians laughed and laughed.

Some of our own best known writers included in the book were not there: John Updike, Raymond Carver, Alice Walker, Mary Gordon, Adrienne Rich, Wendell Berry, Robert Penn Warren, Mary Gordon, John Sales.

Only four American writers accepted the return two-week invitation from the Soviet Writers' Union in May 1990: Sharon Olds, Joyce Johnson (girlfriend of Jack Kerouac at the time *On the Road* was published), F. D. (Frank) Reeve, father of Christopher Reeve, and me, together with our sponsor, Janet Riley, her mother, and others from the Quaker US/USSR Committee. Frank Reeve spoke Russian, which helped.

We were loosely connected to a more illustrious group of American writers selected by Norman Cousins, under a program supported by Pepperdine University. We were with them on some occasions, others not. They were Elizabeth Hardwick, Alfred Kazin, William Gass, Studs Terkel, Louis Auchincloss, David Halberstam, and the late Harrison Salisbury.

But things had changed politically in Russia since the year before. The writers we'd met, and with whom we'd bonded in Washington, were not there to meet us. Two came to see us, bringing books and spirits before we left, but were not at the scheduled conferences.

We were bountifully entertained, however, beginning with private rooms in the Ukraine Hotel, Moscow. Between conferences, we were taken by bus to visit Susdal, by train for two days in Pskov, and by bus to Portvino, the science center, which looked more or less abandoned at the time. In Pskov we visited Pushkin's estate and his tomb. Pushkin is the most beloved of Russian writers by his countrymen. Tolstoy, Chekhov, Dostoevsky, Turgenev, Gogol, are seldom mentioned, Babel not at all.

Of American writers known and read in Russia, there's only Faulkner. Faulkner's books are everywhere books are sold.

The conferences, held in the relatively posh Writers' Union building, were heavy, sometimes stormy. The overall theme, "The Moral Effects of Social Change," gave Russian writers a chance to passionately vent their frustrations. Life in Russia was hard for writers, as for everyone else.

I don't remember whether or not I had to say anything during those sessions. In case I did, I found jotted down in a note-book:

> I live in a different part of the world and a different setting from anyone here, even my American colleagues. . . .
>
> My farm is located 21 miles from Selma, Alabama, so you know that I'm familiar with social change of another sort. My world has been turned upside down in the past two decades, and change seems still to be gathering force. No one seems to know how to cope.
>
> The main thought I have about the moral effect of such change is that increased freedom calls for increased responsibility of a personal nature.
>
> Upon signing the surrender instrument by Japan in 1945, Gen. Douglas MacArthur said that what was called for was a "spiritual recrudescence and improvement of human character." Recrudescence is a word that I would never use, but has such lofty connotation it has stuck in my mind.

Though there was a nationwide food shortage in Russia, we were invited to a sumptuous meal at the poet Yevtushenko's dacha, after which he took us to Pasternak's house and to his grave, where some in the group made speeches. Then we all drank wine and hurled our plastic cups to the ground.

Sharon, Joyce, and I hired a driver to visit Chekhov's house in Moscow one day. We were asked to step into large slides for protection of the floors, but we did more. We took off our shoes in homage.

What I brought home was deep admiration for the people and for the land. The people are strong, intelligent, proud, and poor. Like southerners, they're generally courteous. Our bus driver,

With the poet Yevtushenko, at his dacha in Russia.

upon arrival at a destination, would say, "I invite you to leave the bus," and later, "You are welcome to return to the bus."

They are readers. In Russia our book, *The Human Experience*, sold out, 50,000 copies. At home, less than 6,000 copies were sold. The main problem of our Russian publisher, he told us, was an excess of demand, plus a shortage of paper.

The country landscape is flat and wide, the soil dark and rich like that of the southern Black Belt. There are no billboards. Along the roadsides, tiny peasant houses with gingerbread trim and muted contrasting colors look, from outside, like fairytale houses.

We kept wondering what the houses were like inside, so our Russian leader/driver stopped to ask a farmer if we might go into his house. The first farmer refused, but another generously invited us in.

The ground floor, like a basement, housed two cows. Up the narrow stairs, a kitchen, neat and clean, had equipment as primitive as a century ago at home. In the bedroom, the farmer apologized because the bed was unmade. His wife had left very early for her job, he said. In the other bedroom, a grandmother, frozen with unease, sat holding a young child, also frozen, on her lap. Some of our group offered chewing gum and candy, which the grandmother took without a word or change of expression. The tiny sitting room was sparsely furnished with Sears Roebuck–type furniture.

The farmer told us he was allowed ten acres of land, which he pointed out with pride.

I was so touched by his courtesy and poverty that, back in the bus, I began to cry. This was the way visitors from the North feel when they go into houses of black people at home, I thought. Joyce gave me a piece of hoarded chocolate for comfort.

In the wide fields, old-fashioned haystacks and antiquated farm machinery are picturesque, but indicative of long, hard labor. Birch trees are everywhere.

In the cities, there were no sirens, day or night. I wondered what people did in emergencies. At pay-off counters change was made with an abacus. But the architecture is magnificent, parks are numerous and well kept. In May a pervasive scent of lilacs was everywhere, even upon walking out of our hotel.

The Soviet Union is no more. Politics and demographics have changed completely since 1990. But one element is the same, I'm sure—the soul of the Russian people.

This trip and the previous one to Washington have remained high points in my life. I will always be indebted to the Society of Friends, to Janet Riley, and to Dr. Anthony Manousis who chose my story.

Home again, my house was a wreck, my dog, Boone, in the veterinary clinic with an infected foot. I'd been gone for three weeks and the Practicalities had piled up. I had to have a new septic tank for the house, a breast biopsy that showed no malignancy, and four root canals on one tooth.

But I found Reda Blake, wife of the then-commandant at Marion Institute. Reda was an accountant but not working. One day I heard her say that her favorite time of the month was when she balanced her checkbook. "Then please do mine!" I said. She said that she would and, though she's since moved to Tennessee, has relieved me of that by mail ever since.

And I found Betty Nichols from a nearby Mennonite community. Betty began coming to help me one day a week. In addition to cleaning, straightening, finding lost books and papers, Betty would listen to and criticize my work in progress if there was time. She brought homemade bread, plus food that we put together with mine to share at a lunchtime break. She became a very special friend.

Reda and Betty make it possible for me to manage here alone.

With my new blueberry-blue iMac computer and laser printer, I should have been able to write better and faster. But since I have no basic understanding of computers, I couldn't solve problems that stopped me for variable periods of time. Freeze after freeze was caused by a faulty mouse that no one suspected. I couldn't transfer work to a diskette because the diskette holder had never been connected.

Kirtley pere had a joking explanation for such deficiencies. The Lord made me on a Saturday afternoon when He was tired, Kirtley said. He had several leftover parts too good to throw away, so He decided to make one more and quit. A few of the usual parts weren't there, however, so He simply left them out and hoped for the best.

As before, there were few worked-and-walked days. I don't

know whether I was seduced by continuing attention from my native state, mired down in Practicalities, or simply feeling my age, which was now over seventy. For whatever reason, stories were always in my mind and partially on the computer, but I couldn't seem to get them finished.

From 1986 to 1991, I'd written only three new stories, "The Birthday Cake," "A New Life," and "A Meeting on the Road."

Before I considered a story finished, it had to hold my own attention without a thought-break from beginning to end. Now I worked more slowly than ever. Each morning I'd go over what I'd written the day before, beginning with the first sentence, like a sergeant inspecting his squad. If a word stopped me, even for an instant, it was reconsidered, usually changed, often after a trip to the thesaurus. "Show, don't tell" is the short story caveat, so most adjectives had to go. And my old journalistic training always kicked in to delete all unnecessary words, especially the *and's, but's,* and *the's.* I didn't want a reader to have to read a sentence of mine twice, since I very much appreciated its being read the first time.

I was further slowed down by the desire not to disappoint the readers I already had. I wanted to do better than before, wanted Crawford to read a story and say, "It's the best thing you've done." He never did. He loved the first draft of "The Birthday Cake," but I insisted that it wasn't finished and kept adding and subtracting until I almost wrote it to death.

When it was finally accepted by the *Threepenny Review*, I wrote the editor, Wendy Lesser, Dec. 18, 1990:

> This story is a whole year's work, and then some. When my two readers here read the first draft, long ago, they were enthusiastic and all praise. But the more I worked on it, the more silent they became. They had thought it was funny, and it wasn't any more. I

wanted it to be funny but serious, too. So the funeral kept getting better and the rest of it worse. They had no suggestions. Just that silence. Finally, I thought it was maybe as good as I could get it and sent it to Binky Urban, my agent, who sent it out. *The New Yorker* said the tone was so flat it deadened the story. It was rejected by *Harper's, Lear's, McCall's,* and finally *Story.* At that point, I asked Binky not to send it out again until I'd done something to it.

So I worked on it two more months, at least. At some time in there, I was scheduled to read in Tuscaloosa, and decided to read the story. I told the audience I'd welcome suggestions. As I read, the funeral seemed to go on and on to me. When it was over, one woman said, "In 'The Amaryllis' you kept referring to the plant. Maybe you should mention the cake more often." I couldn't refer to the cake, but I could spread out the information about Fern's marriage all through the funeral, and keep entering her mind. After that finally dawned on me, it was a matter of getting the words right and Fern-like.

So I hope it works now, and that your readers will like it. If it's successful, it could be a textbook case in revision.

There were still acceptances and speeches, which I first had to write. So I seemed to spend more time on speeches than on stories. In 1991, *Tongues* received the Lillian Smith Award for Fiction from the Southern Regional Council, and I read the following acceptance in Atlanta. KW took me.

When Dr. Norell called to tell me, he asked first if I knew who Lillian Smith was. Almost everyone of my generation knew Lillian Smith for her famous, best-selling novel, *Strange Fruit.* Since then, I had thought of her more in connection with civil rights than with literature.

Being a jazz aficionado, I came to associate "Strange Fruit" with Billie Holliday and a song that she made famous, the song with which she liked to close her performances. I assumed that she got the title from the book. Now I find that both song and book titles came from an unknown poet who sent the lyrics to Billie in protest of lynchings in the South. Billie recorded the song before the book came out.

Originally, Ms. Smith had given her book manuscript the title *Jordan Is So Chilly*. When asked by her publisher to look for something better, she chose *Strange Fruit*, but with reservations. She thought that linking the novel with a song about a lynching distorted the theme of the book. In her view, *Strange Fruit* was about more than a lynching. It was about the strange fruit of a racist culture.

She spent most of her life trying to change that culture.

So when I accept this award in her name, I feel like something of an imposter. As Chekhov once said in the face of acclaim he thought he didn't deserve, "I feel like a scoundrel."

Writers of fiction are not so much participants, certainly not movers and shakers, as observers and recorders. To be both doer and truth-teller (different from reporter) is like trying to serve both God and Mammon, two gods.

The primary concerns of a fiction writer are not ideas or causes but people. The subject of this conference is Democracy. I must confess that when I think of that word and the grandeur of its implications, I want to be in the back row of the audience. A fiction writer's consuming interest is in people, in what they say and do, and why they say and do it. Consciously or unconsciously, he or she never gets away from this born fascination.

Writer after fiction writer has attested to this predilection, shortcoming, whatever. Not the least of these was William Faulkner, whom Ms. Smith didn't like. According to her biographer, Anne

Loveland, she regarded him as a talented writer of fiction, but said that "he was not an intellectual . . . not a thinker . . . not mature psychologically and socially." She admitted that he said some good things on the race problem, but he was at best, and only since receiving the Nobel Prize, a "mighty lukewarm liberal."

As for Faulkner, he said repeatedly that what the fiction writer is trying to do is to create living people, in conflict with their own hearts, their fellows, or their environment. "I am writing about people, not ideas or symbols," he said time after time in taped interviews at the University of Virginia. He said he tried to make his characters "whole, intact, breathing, and standing up," with no judgement on the author's part whatsoever. A fiction writer is not interested in bettering man's condition, he said. He's interested in man's behavior. "His job is to tell what man will do, not what he should do. Maybe what he can't help doing. . . ."

I would say, in addition, that if what the characters do should illuminate a certain human landscape so that improvements result, as in the case of Dickens and his novels, it's all to the good but incidental.

This could be viewed as a copout, except that if the fiction succeeds, it becomes art. And art is the great sustainer of mankind in all his struggles.

The late John Gardner, in his book titled *On Moral Fiction*, defines morality as "nothing more than doing what is unselfish, helpful, kind, and noble-hearted." He goes on to say that great art celebrates life's potential, offering a vision unmistakably and unsentimentally rooted in love. . . .

By love I think he means the simple but acute appreciation of being alive, of having the opportunity to walk on this earth, to know and care about other human beings, animals, or even a place.

I think it has to be tough love, though, and the vision has to be true. That's the hard part, seeing and telling the truth. For the truth has more than one aspect, as in the case of a divorce. Learning to see and tell the truth is the work of a life, and of a *lifetime.*

So back to the lives of two gifted women, one a writer, the other a singer, both indelibly associated with a phrase, "Strange Fruit," and all of its connotations. Both women gave their all, one to her art (Billie loved being called an "artist," as she was in England), the other primarily to a cause, as I see it.

Now Columbia Records has just released the ninth and final CD of "The Quintessential Billie Holliday." According to Whitney Balliat in the *New Yorker,* "It is now possible to see the whole beautiful and invaluable Billy Holliday landscape of the thirties." Later, sadder years are available on Decca and Verve recordings. Lillian Smith is also still very much alive, for what she wrote and what she did. Her best books, notably *Killers of the Dream,* are still in print and still being read. Here today she is memorialized by this group for the twenty-fourth time, with two awards, one of which I am honored to receive.

Interviews were usually done over the phone, but some were written. On one, for the twelfth-grade Advanced Placement English Class, Gadsden High School, I spent considerable time. Their questions were so good I include a couple of answers, in which the questions are implicit.

I put some white on the black dog because things are seldom black or white, but a mixture. I suppose I made the dog young because his death would be more poignant young than old. It was not a conscious decision.

When I wrote the story I wasn't thinking of race at all. But when I sent it to my agent, that was the first thing that occurred to him. He doubted that he could sell the story for that reason, and he was right. I meant the story to be about the limits of human responsibility. How many needs, animal or human, can a person take on in addition to his own, and still surive?

In "Tongues of Flame," my idea was that E. L. went back to the church for the cigarettes he'd put in the collection plate. He didn't mean to set the church on fire. Being on the religious hot-seat all those nights was too much for him. He was probably dead drunk when he went back to Rehobeth, too drunk to be fooling with matches. I don't think he returned Dovey's affection. He was too sick and too lost. Maybe setting the church on fire was a turning point. But I left him for good, there in the church yard, passed out under the tree.

In 1992 Libba Buchanan called to tell me that hardback copies of *Tongues* were remaindered on Hamilton Bookseller's list for $1.00 each, And Binky called with the news that 1800 paperbacks were about to be pulped by Pocket Books.

The University of Alabama Press came to the rescue. Jerry Elijah Brown, then head of the Auburn University Department of Journalism, wrote a much appreciated introduction, and the University of Alabama Press brought out a handsome paperback *Tongues* in its Library of Alabama Classics, reprint editions that won't be allowed to go out of print.

Binky called, Jan. 5, 1994, to say that Sam had died. Her news was followed by a letter from Houghton Mifflin, where he'd moved from Dutton. I'd come to dearly love him. He'd recently signed a gift book, "May we both go on together for years to come." Another time he signed, "Your publisher for life." He'd given me a leather-bound copy of *Tongues*, for which he'd chosen the end papers, and he wrote, "I hope you'll give me an opportunity to do it again."

So I'd lost both publisher and friend.

Over the years, in my Week At A Glance calendars, there were the same refrains. Urinary tract infections. Flares of arthritis. Ordering clothes from mail-order catalogs, sending them back, or having them altered by Mabel Carroll at Nathan Harris' Sons, Marion.

And there were wonderful times with my granddaughters. "Children to supper, soup, sandwiches. Made gingerbread after." "Children for Valentines. Gumbo and Irish Soda bread"; "Children to spend night. Watched 'Murder She Wrote' Wonderful time"; "Children to shop Dollar Store and Bargain Town"; "Children to spend night. Eye-of-the-round for supper."

And later "To Selma birthday shopping for M. H. and Helen. Two outfits each." Still later in high school, "Got ready for girls. They didn't come." Their lives branched out farther and farther. Mary Hays went to Knox College, Galesburg, Illinois, Helen to Emory and Henry, Abingdon, Virginia.

In time there was high blood pressure and finding the right medicine to control it. Deafness came and grew worse, with the need for hearing aids and a barking dog.

Kirtley and I had always had dogs, and I'd always had one or two dogs since he died. I needed a dog for companionship as well as for protection. "You have to have something that *breathes*," a widow friend once told me.

Boone, a German shorthaired pointer, was perhaps the best dog I ever had. A Selma realtor, Deans Barber Jr., gave him to me because he was gun shy. KW and I went to pick him up in KW's jeep. He got into the jeep without urging. At home, we penned him up for a day or two, and when I let him out he didn't try to leave.

He was content outside in the yard or lying by my computer for hours while I worked. On the back seat of the car, he went with me everywhere that I went.

But he was a hunting dog, and occasionally took off to hunt for several days, coming back limping and exhausted.

He was with me until he was old, deaf, and couldn't get up and down the stairs. Then he spent nights and most of his days on an L.L. Bean dog pad in the kitchen, getting up at mid-morning to go out and check the neighborhood.

One day he went out as usual. Helen was here for lunch. He wasn't back when she left, so I began to call, then look. I called KW and Susannah, called the neighbors. We hunted on foot and in cars. Janice Williams rode the area on horseback, and we never found a clue as to what became of him.

People said that good dogs, feeling the approach of death, sometimes go off to die alone. But I never saw buzzards gathered at a spot to suggest it. Since he was still beautiful and didn't look old, I think someone picked him up in a truck and stole him, which sometimes happens to dogs in the country.

I've always grieved to think he didn't have the good end he deserved, and that his collar doesn't hang on my sleeping porch wall with those of other dogs I've had and loved: McArthur, the pointer, Sally Bowles, the weimaraner, Little Sister, the beagle, and Beaudreaux, the English pointer who spent his first two years in a New York City apartment.

I had few cats because dogs don't like them, and because I didn't want them in the house. But I had Little Thing, shortened to Thingy, who appeared on a tree outside the kitchen window. She always knew where I was upstairs, and often slept on the roof outside the window while I worked. When she was ready to have kittens she came up and meowed, so I went down, made a birthing place on the back porch, and stayed with her until three kittens were born.

Families of birds live here, cardinals, chickadees, redbellied woodpeckers, doves. Indigo buntings visit for several weeks each summer. They all eat and bathe outside the breakfast room windows, where I usually eat lunch and supper. And since birdland is a democracy, cowbirds and jaybirds come too. I feed and water them. Betty scrubs out the birdbaths when she comes on Fridays.

Sometimes I have wild animals. Racoons, skunks (called polecats), o'possums, and always armadillos. A fox once killed the guineas that I had. Fire ants build their dirt pyramids all over the yard. To step on one is to be hurtfully bitten.

And the Practicalities never let up. My new pump was struck by lightening. The roof had to be replaced, the front porch painted, and, after I slipped and sprained an ankle, side rails put up on the steps. I had a bone infection in my foot, which couldn't be diagnosed for months. With one shoe on, the other in a cast to the knee, I did a scheduled reading in the Brewton Library. KW took me to that one.

Sometimes a Practicality would take weeks, even months, to deal with. The Southern Natural Gas Company wanted to come across the Cahaba River place for the third time. It meant another large pipe under the ground. No landowner wants it across his or her place. It takes up a wide strip of farmland with imposing metal structures along the way. It had already ruined our beautiful sand bar.

But the Gas Company does have to pay, and its goal is to pay as little as possible. The landowner's goal is to get every possible cent short of a condemnation. The last time, with KW's help, I did very well, so I bought a needed new car, an Oldsmobile Cutlass.

When I went for a final lunch with the Gas Company's negotiator, he said, "Is that the car I bought?" It was.

I wanted to be a good citizen, so occasionally took a stand on a public issue. Once (can't find the date), it was to protest a proposed landfill to be located southeast of Marion, near Suttle.

> My name is Mary T. Ward Brown, of the Hamburg Community. I've lived there, in Perry County, for almost seventy-six years.
>
> I want to go on record as opposing the proposed landfill. I'm not into politics, nor the member of any kind of clique. This is my personal view of the situation tonight.
>
> We have a critical waste disposal problem. This landfill was someone's idea of how to solve it. The idea was carried farther, much farther, by political means which were not open and above-board. People didn't know about the landfill until it was almost a done deal.
>
> But someone found out, and a few citizens rose up to protest. The first to protest, naturally, were those whose homes, churches, and graveyards would be *in* the landfill. Thankfully, they finally woke up the rest of us.
>
> So tonight we're here, and the Perry County Commission will vote on the landfill tomorrow. If I understand rightly, the issue has now become not only political (all the way to Montgomery), but also racial. The three black commissioners are said to be *for* the landfill, the two white commissioners against it.
>
> I would remind the commissioners that when they vote tomorrow, they will be adding to the ongoing history of Perry County, for better or worse. They will exercise their power over all of its people. The power they exercise, and the history they make, will be on a small scale, but they would do well to think of power exercised unwisely on the grand scale.
>
> Power is dangerous. People who abuse it listen to their own

voices, not the voice of the people nor the voice of reason. If our commissioners bring this landfill to Perry County, after all the warnings and sincere protests they've heard, they will do it, in my opinion, to their lasting regret and shame.

To stop the landfill won't solve the waste disposal problem, but there has to be an alternative less negative and hazardous than the proposal before us tonight.

There were many protests and the landfill was defeated at the time. Several years later, protests couldn't stop a very large landfill now located near Uniontown in Perry County.

I was to receive the Governor's Award for the Arts in 1993 but had a urinary tract infection. I was taking the antibiotic, septra, which I'd taken so many times I'd become allergic to it. My doctor had to give me a shot to unswell my face before I could go.

The year 1995 was the seventieth anniversary of Flannery O'Conner's birth, and I was asked, with others, to write a tribute for the *Flannery O'Conner Bulletin*, edited each year by Sarah Gordon at Georgia College & State University, Milledgeville, Georgia.

I wrote the following:

I remember, the way I remember the day President Kennedy was shot, the first time I read a story by Flannery O'Conner. It was in 1953 when southern women had cooks. Together, my cook Hattie Smith and I had cooked and served a typical noonday farm meal of meat, fresh vegetables, hot bread, and homemade dessert. A morning's work.

I took Hattie home and came back for an hour of rest. With me was the new issue of *Harper's Bazaar*, which published fiction at the time. The story I read was "A Late Encounter With The Enemy."

I was electrified. When I saw the word gulls for girls, I felt a stab of pure envy. No writer had penned down southern speech in that way. The characters were so real, familiar, funny, and tragic that I felt present at Sally Poker Sash's graduation, saw the General on the stage in his wheelchair, the irresponsible Boy Scout behind him. At the end, the General was disposed of with two words, *the corpse*. Brilliant, I thought.

Since I'm neither critic nor scholar, I didn't take the story apart or go into its meaning. I simply loved it. And I felt that Flannery O'Conner had split contemporary American fiction into some kind of Before and After.

I had only one doubt that day. Could she do it again? I watched for her work everywhere, followed her career with consuming interest. When she died, I knew that her work would not die with her.

I thought I knew the stories fairly well, but when I read "Late Encounter" again, then some of the less anthologized stories that I only half-remembered, I found that I knew little more than the surface of her work. This time I got, in a personal way, the hard underlying religious message, and it's scary. She gave us fictional prophets because she was a prophet.

In stories like "The Comforts of Home" and "The Partridge Festival," her message seems a little forced to me now, though it feels almost blasphemous to say so. She pushes to incredible extremes, but her genius sweeps the reader along unblinking as people have fits in a doctor's office, get beaten on the back over fresh tattoos, have mystical experiences while hosing down a pig parlor.

How could I have let her books sit on my shelves, even beside Faulkner, Joyce, Flaubert, where I keep them, all this time? I'm reading her again, trying to learn to write fiction and to save my soul!

In 1996, at a foreclosure sale, I bought two and a half acres and a doublewide trailer diagonally across the road from my house. I hoped to find someone to help me, or at least a close neighbor to call on in an emergency. So far I've had neighbors but no one to help.

The Society for the Fine Arts, The University of Alabama, gave me the Distinguished Career Award for 1997. I wrote and read the following acceptance:

Before Dr. Sorensen wrote me of this award, I don't think I'd consciously thought of myself as having a career. It's true that I'd worked as a writer, off and on, to the limit of my ability, for many years. But before that, I was a housewife for thirty-one years, and it's hard to change a self-image.

On occasion, though, another image would emerge. For instance, all my life I'd wanted to serve on a jury, but had never been selected because both my brother and my son practiced law in Perry County where I live. Once, though, I had a summons to Federal Court in Dallas County, and my hopes soared. Mrs. McCrummin, wife of the president of Judson College, was also summoned. When the lawyers questioned the venire, one lawyer asked Mrs. McCrummin what her occupation was. "I'm a housewife," she said. I thought that was so modest and dear, because she's a musician, a professional organist and pianist, a music teacher.

But when my turn came, I'd been thinking ahead. This was a drug case, and I figured they'd think a housewife might have a closed mind. I really wanted to be on that jury. So when the lawyer asked my occupation, I said, "Fiction writer."

"I didn't get that," the lawyer said.

"Fiction writer," I said, louder, and he wrote it down.

We were both selected, Mrs. McCrummin and I. But the case was settled out of court, so I still haven't served on a jury.

Writing was what I always wanted to do, though, even when I was totally absorbed in other things. And in a way, I think I was always getting ready, just in case. Mainly by reading (probably the best way we learn to write) and by storing up what we call "material." Everyone does it, makes a collection of interesting incidents, characters, and facts. But writers do it for a purpose.

The purpose in fiction is not to nail down material as in autobiography or history, but to play with it and change it in the mind, or more accurately, to work on it. The writer's imagination is like a large work room filled with any and everything from the world as he knows it—blocks of experience heavy as wood, broken icons, faces with and without masks, secrets (the best material of all), a thousand trinkets, one or two real gemstones, and junk. From this the writer sets out to make something beautiful, he hopes, or at least interesting.

Why? Because he was born with a troubling instinct to create with words. And more than that, to share what he knows and thinks and feels. To share his humanity. He hopes to make the reader think, of what he's written, "Yes, that's true," or "Yes, that was inevitable."

It's more nearly a calling than a career. Most of us are endowed with small talent, not genius, and whether we manage to tap into the great universal or not doesn't signify. The goal and the effort sustain us.

The next month I did a "lectureship" at Spring Hill College, Mobile. I was to teach a class, but my written lecture on *The Sound and the Fury* didn't fill up the time. The students didn't talk as I expected, so Dr. John Hafner, of the English faculty, who was sitting in, saved the session. Later, I read "A Meeting on the Road" for the first time, which went better than the class, and there was a fine reception and book signing after. Dr. Margaret Davis was the coordinator.

Meanwhile, the few stories I'd written were being published. "The Birthday Cake" and "A Meeting on the Road," in *Threepenny Review*, Berkeley, California; "A New Life," *The Atlantic Monthly*; "It Wasn't All Dancing," Grand Street, New York City; "In a Foreign Country," *Five Points*, Georgia State University, Atlanta; "Once In A Lifetime," *Many Voices, Many Rooms*, The University of Alabama.

And some of the new stories, plus others from *Tongues*, were being included in anthologies: *The Christ-Haunted Landscape: Faith and Doubt in Southern Fiction*, edited by Susan Ketchin; *God Stories*, edited by C. Michael Curtis; *New Stories from the South*, edited by Shannon Ravenel; *Songs of Experience: An Anthology on Growing Old*, edited by Margaret Fowler and Priscilla McCutcheon; *New Stories by Southern Women*, edited by Mary Ellis Gibson; *Stories: Contemporary Southern Short Fiction*, edited by Donald Hays; *Downhome: An Anthology of Southern Women Writers*, edited by Susie Mee; *Alabama Bound: Contemporary Stories of a State*, edited by James E. Colquitt; *A New Life: Stories and Photographs from the Suburban South*, edited by Alex Harris with Alice Rose George.

Binky called in 1998 and told me to send the stories I considered good enough for a new collection, so that she could look for a publisher. I sent eight plus "The Newcomers' Tea," which I've never been able to get right. She sent them out once and gave up. There weren't enough, and some weren't good enough.

She also sent me a book, by a client she thought I should read. It was *All the Pretty Horses* by Cormac McCarthy, which I read, as I wrote her, "with awe." I think McCarthy is one of the few, if not the only, American writer working now whose work will endure. His prose is so wonderful it can take a reader through subject matter from which he or she might normally recoil.

But I *wasn't* writing stories. I'd worked on two, but kept putting them aside to write speeches and do readings. In a neglected workbook, I described a dream I'd had the night before. I was driving down a country road when my car suddenly went into reverse. Brake and emergency brakes were both gone. I was frantically shifting gears, turning off the ignition, hopelessly trying to keep the car on the road and out of a ditch, while going backward faster and faster until I woke up. I thought it could be a message from my subconscious, reminding me that my work was going backward.

But I came to know, and spend time with, exceptional people with roots in the Black Belt. Dr. William Hurt Sledge, from Greensboro, Master Professor of Psychiatry at Yale, introduced me to the late, great Samuel Mockbee, affectionately known as Sambo, who'd started The Rural Studio for the Auburn University School of Architecture. It was a bold, original concept of hands-on teaching in my neighboring Hale County. And there was Dr. Virginia Saft (now Monde), a Chicago psychoanalyst, who maintained her family home in Greensboro. She read *Tongues of Flame* in Chicago and, on subsequent visits to Greensboro, became a friend.

I met William Christenberry, a preeminent American photographer, who came from the Black Belt. When he was honored in Greensboro with a special William Christenberry Day, I was asked to read in the amazing Tire Chapel, built largely of leftover truck and automobile tires, by Sambo's students.

11

IT WASN'T ALL DANCING

SINCE I COULDN'T SEEM to finish new stories, I began going through old ones. A few were worth rewriting, I thought, and was surprised to find how much I'd learned about writing fiction since I started so long ago.

And one day early in the new century, 2000, Curtis Clark, editor of the University of Alabama Press, called to say he'd heard that I had a number of stories toward a collection, and that he'd like to see them.

So Binky sent him the ten stories we considered acceptable. He didn't like two, so I rewrote what came to be "A Good Heart" and "The Parlor Tumblers." And he decided to include a short memoir, "Swing Low," recently published in *The Remembered Gate*, by the University of Alabama Press. So he settled on ten stories and the memoir.

They had to be passed on by several readers and finally the Board of Directors which, in January 2001, approved the publication.

Finally, struggling with a new computer program, Microsoft Word 98, I got the stories on diskettes and sent them off to Curtis. Next came a long questionnaire, which I called "The Q," to be filled in. I finally mailed it to Beth Motherwell, the marketing manager, who became a special new friend.

By March I was reading a copyedited manuscript of the new

book, and on November 26, 2001, ten copies of *It Wasn't All Dancing* arrived in the mail. I was eighty-four.

Readings and signings began first at the Sturdivant Hall Gift Shop in Selma, December 12. In early January 2002, they resumed in earnest. Crosshaven Books, Birmingham; Capital Books, Montgomery; the Greensboro Library; the Selma Library; all the places I'd read before. I was also scheduled to go back to Mississippi, to Jackson and Oxford.

For that trip, and from then on, I'd acquired three travel companions, all college English professors from Montgomery. Dr. Richard Anderson (Rick), retired, Huntingdon College, was the driver, always in a sporty *new* red car. His wife, Nancy, Auburn University, Montgomery, a woman of many praiseworthy passions, literary and social, was the coordinator. Dr. Susie Paul, also of AUM, an inspiring teacher and poet, was my roommate and guardian.

For later trips, when Nancy and Susie were teaching, Rick took me. When he couldn't go, Susie drove me in my ordinary gray Oldsmobile.

After Mississippi, Rick took me in February to read twice for a conference at Calhoun Community College, Decatur, planned and directed by the English teacher, Dr. Randy Cross. I read twice in one day in Auburn, in the morning for Dr. Flynt's history class and in the late afternoon at Pebble Hill, now the beautifully renovated (by her children) Caroline Marshall Draughon Center for the Arts and Humanities. There was a day with Judith Patterson, author of *Sweet Memories*, at Judson.

Soon after, I woke up one morning with a complete loss of balance. Falling first over my bedside table, I couldn't stand or walk without falling. I had to be taken downstairs on a stretcher and to ER in an ambulance. After a week in the hospital, there were three more weeks of therapy "to regain my center of gravity" in the Perry County Nursing Home. Final diagnosis, an inner ear disturbance.

Back home, I wrote in my little week-at-a-glance calendar, "Happy to be well again, in my own house with all my books and stuff."

And by May I was able to go to Monroeville to receive the Harper Lee Award for 2002. I read the following:

Since you're now a captive audience, I'd like to say a few words, personal and nonpersonal, about the difficulties of being a writer, especially the difficulties of being, in one lifetime, a good writer and a good person.

By good person I don't mean Citizen of the Year, United Way chairman, or Sunday School teacher, all highly praiseworthy, but simply someone who can go to bed at night with a sense of satisfaction, not frustration or regret because he or she has chosen to be a writer.

A person like William Faulkner, born with genius, has little choice. He writes. He has to write, no matter what. Tolstoy, on the other hand, born with perhaps greater genius, tore his family apart and eventually ruined his art, in an effort to choose between writing and something he thought to be of higher value. He struggled until the day he died, in a borrowed room of the stationmaster's cottage in an obscure railway station, to which he'd fled his problems.

Most of us, though, are born not with genius but mere talent. My own talent is so small that whatever I've accomplished has come more from hard work and the drive to write well than from any gift of nature. Writers like me have to make choices, sometimes sacrifices.

Virginia Wolfe said that to be a writer, a woman must have money and a room of her own, which has to be true for men as well. The problem is, where does the money come from, and the room? Most of us have to earn them, usually with full-time jobs.

So if we work and write on the side, or vice versa, what time do we have for family, social and community life, or visible service like Meals on Wheels or tutoring a child? We're constantly squeezing time from one place to fill up another, and the time we squeeze is usually time we consider our own—our writing time, unless we're money-makers, which most of us aren't and never will be.

For me, writing becomes obsessive. When I'm working, I don't want to stop except to eat and sleep. My unconscious prayer is something like "Deliver me from everything and everybody except this." But an old friend comes to town, calls up, and wants to come for a visit. Someone dies, like Sadie in my story "The Birthday Cake." Someone has surgery. It's Christmas, Easter, Labor Day.

So what do we do? If we say no, or yes and don't show up, people who don't write don't understand. How could they? White lies are no solution. To shed a situation or an acquaintance who's leaching our time is so painful we wish we hadn't done it. We think less of ourselves, think we're not a good person. And to sleep well at night we need a self-image we can live with in reasonable comfort.

I admit that I've never learned to cope with such choices except on an impromptu basis.

I do know that writing is a chancy business. Little, if anything, of what people like me produce will outlive the present. I've always had the daunting feeling that my own work would probably wind up book by book in a Good Will store, priced ten cents, and I actually did find a first edition of *Tongues of Flame* at a book sale for $1.00. Tillie Olsen, who, in the sixties, wrote a few brilliant stories, such as "Tell Me A Riddle" and "I Stand Here Ironing," was widely praised and anthologized. Young readers of today never heard of her. Writers, even good writers, are here today, gone tomorrow.

"Follow your bliss," Joseph Campbell, the mythologist told his adherents. Writing is my bliss. Since I didn't grow up in a literary family and have never lived, except briefly, in a literary community, I didn't discover this bliss as early as some. Once I found it, though, I've followed faithfully but in a zigzag fashion. When I wasn't able to write, I read, listened, tried to learn as much as possible about literature and life, and allowed myself to feel whatever was to be felt.

There's a wonderful true story told and recorded by Isak Dinesen, who wrote *Seven Gothic Tales* and *Out of Africa*. She introduces herself as one of an "ancient tribe of wild idle people who have sat down among honest hardworking folks of the real world to create another kind of reality." She calls her story "The King's Letter." During the time she lived in Africa, the story goes, she sent the skin of a fine lion she'd killed back to the King of Denmark, her native country. The King wrote her a letter of thanks, which she happened to have in her pocket when, riding the farm one day, she came upon one of her native workers on the side of the road with a crushed and broken leg. His pain was almost unbearable. She chose to sit with him until his native companion could go on foot to find transportation to a hospital.

During the long wait, he kept begging for something to ease his pain. She had nothing she could give him except a few lumps of sugar, which seemed to help a little but soon gave out.

Then, as he cried and begged for help, she thought of the King's letter. She told him yes, she did have something excellent. She had a letter from a king, and everyone knew that a letter from a king, in his own hand, would do away with pain, however bad. So she placed the letter on his chest, and it really did help and seem to ease his pain all the way to the hospital. Thereafter, mystical power was attributed to the letter, and it was borrowed to ease the pain of natives on her farm for as long as she lived in Africa.

She ends the story like this: "We who call ourselves, or feel ourselves to be, servants of the word, in looking at it, will see, each of us, as I do, the wish that something we have written, that I have written, by my own hand may at some time, in some place, to people in need be The King's Letter.

At the conference I met Pam Kingsbury, an English teacher, the University of North Alabama, Florence, and book reviewer (*Inner Voices, Inner Views*), wife and caretaker of the legendary, tragically ill UNA professor, Jack Kingsbury. (He died in 2008.) She became a friend with whom I stay in regular touch.

Since I wanted to encourage new ventures in the arts, and especially anything done by Sam Mockbee's students, I went later in May to the ribbon-cutting ceremony for a pavilion built by five Rural Studio Students. It was the grand opening of Perry Lakes Park, 2002, and I read the following:

This beautiful pavilion, and the five young architects who built it, bring to mind a magical word. Possibility. The pavilion is a possibility fulfilled.

Alfred North Whitehead, the British philosopher, once wrote, "Our minds are finite, and yet even in these circumstances of finitude we are surrounded by possibilities that are infinite, and the purpose of human life is to grasp as much as we can out of that infinitude."

I hope this structure, conceived and built by the hard work and high purpose of these young artists, will be a lasting inspiration to each of us here, to the citizens of Perry County, and to all who come here to enjoy the beauty of nature and an example of human accomplishment.

On my eighty-fifty birthday the next month, 2002, I was honored with a beautiful candlelit dinner at the home of my friends,

Buffy and Brandon Taylor, in Marion.

Once I tried to promote a personal cause. I thought Drucilla Collins McCollum, a matron at Judson during my student days, should be included in the Alabama Women's Hall of Fame. Headed by her niece, Gwen Turner of Demopolis, we began the promotion too late, it seems, so the cause has failed so far. But I go on believing she should be there. I include my letter of July 11, 2002, to the executive secretary, Connie Cook:

I write to endorse the nomination of Drucilla Collins McCollum to the Alabama Women's Hall of Fame. It is my conviction that if anyone ever deserved to be there, it is Mrs. McCollum.

She was a matron at Judson College, in charge of the college laundry, when I was a student there from 1934 to 1938. She addressed each of us as "daughter," though she probably knew our names, and was probably the most beloved and respected person on the entire college staff. We called her "Mrs. Mack."

In those days black laundresses took care of the students' laundry. They came to the dormitory rooms, picked up the laundry, and took it to their homes. Then they brought it back, washed and pressed. Mrs. Mack was in charge of the laundresses and their assignments, and dealt with all the complications that came with the job. She handled it all with the grace and kindness she showed to everyone, everywhere.

We knew that she had been a longtime missionary, that her husband had died, and that at his funeral she had walked down the aisle of the church with a smile on her face. We knew that she was a living testimony to her faith, though I don't think I ever heard her speak of it.

She made such an impression on me that I later wrote a short story using her as model for the main character. The story title is

"No Spring Nor Summer Beauty," from a poem by William Butler Yeats, with the quote, "No spring nor summer beauty hath such grace, as I have seen in one autumnal face." In the story, the main character, who is also a matron in a girls' school, is referred to as "a saint in residence."

I understand that someone else (her niece, Gwen Turner, Demopolis) has sent her professional credentials. I send this as testimony to her lasting influence on hundreds of Judson women over the years, and in the hope that she will be memorialized in the Alabama Women's Hall of Fame as she so richly deserves.

In September, Susie took me to read at the Bay Minette Library. We spent the night with Bobbie and Tom Meacham in the large, Victorian-style house they'd built in Perdido. It was a mini-vacation for me. After the reading, I slept until past noon the next day in Bobbie's quiet guestroom.

The next year, 2003, was busy. I was now eighty-six. In January I wrote and read a forty-five-minute speech at the Mobile Public Library, to which my friend, Beth Motherwell of the UAP, took me. We ate lunch at Wintzell's and stayed at the Admiral Simms Hotel. The reading was followed by a reception, where the entire Judson alumnae chapter, headed by Elizabeth Lee Vignes, my old Hamburg playmate, came to support me. "We'll all be there to clap!" she said. My friend, Anne Inge, Kirtley's godmother, with two of her friends, took us to the Bienville Club for dinner.

The next month Susie took me to Southern Voices 2003 at the Hoover Public Library, an outstanding yearly conference. Roger Rosenblatt was the star that year, and I had a chance to meet two rising young southern writers, Silas House and Ron Rash. I read the same Mobile speech, cut down to thirty minutes.

And in April, Rick took me back to Mobile to receive the Alabama Library Association Award for fiction for the second time. I read the following acceptance:

> This is a memorable occasion for me, because you did me the same honor in 1987 when my first book, *Tongues of Flame*, was published. The Alabama Library Award for Fiction was the first award I ever received, and the plaque you gave me hangs on my workroom wall today. I hope none of you remember how unprepared and speechless I was back then. I would be speechless this time as well, if I hadn't learned in the meantime to put my thoughts on paper beforehand.
>
> I do sincerely thank you. Again.
>
> Libraries, it seems to me, are the unsung heroes of our literary life. Bookstores and writers are programmed to sell books, the bookstores for their own survival and writers for the survival of their publishers. But when the tours and signings are over, it's the libraries that house our books and keep them alive, often longer than they deserve to be on a life-support system.
>
> Not only that, but Alabama libraries promote us all over the state with programs such as "Read Alabama," "Alabama Voices," and that magnificent yearly conference at the Hoover Public Library called, this year, "Southern Voices." You host us locally with readings and signings. In my own area, the Selma Public Library holds regular literary study groups led by AUM professors, one of whose husband, Dr. Rick Anderson, was good enough to bring me down here today. The Selma Library also hosts monthly authors' luncheons with readings and signings by visiting writers. Last September your own John Sledge was there with his beautiful book, *Cities of Silence*. He gave one of the best programs I've ever attended. The Marion–Perry County Library has developed a popular genealogy section with its own computer, nonliterary, but much used by the public;

and the newly opened Uniontown Library has an interesting program called "Mother Reading," for teaching young mothers how to read to their children. Then, for one lucky writer, the Greensboro Library has a fabulous tea each spring, an extravaganza of garden flowers and homemade refreshments. And finally libraries lend us perpetually to all who don't care to buy us.

I live in the country, which in my childhood was eight miles of unpaved prairie roads to the nearest town, so I missed the opportunity of access to a library. And since my first five years of schooling were in a two-room school called the Blackbelt Consolidated Academy, which had no library, the first one with which I was familiar was at Perry County High School in the sixth grade. Sadly, though, I remember it primarily as the place for study hall. Outside of class, I was always working on the high school newspaper, the only opportunity I had for writing at the time, and writing was a thing to which I'd been irresistibly drawn for as long as I can remember. I do recall discovering and reading Joseph Conrad in that library, and I do remember something I've always loved about libraries, flowers on the librarian's desk.

During my years at Judson, the library seemed to be mainly a place for reference. I'd rush over, look something up, make notes, and rush back to the dorm. There, as in high school, I was always at work on the newspaper. I seem to have done very little extracurricular reading while I was in school.

But when I married and moved to Auburn, I thought I'd found heaven itself in what is now the Ralph Brown Draughon Library. By then I'd read *Look Homeward, Angel* and had fallen in love with Thomas Wolfe, and I remember reading down that long shelf of his works until I was saturated with his words, his angst, and his improvisations on chosen themes. I enjoyed that library to the full until we moved back to the country where I'd been born and raised, where my husband died in 1970, and where I still live today. Though the roads have long been paved and straightened, it is still six miles to the nearest library, and I don't get there as often as I'd like.

One of my limitations as a writer has been a lack of scholarship and range of information. My interests have been self-limiting rather than expanded by exposure, and my work suffers from a kind of intellectual malnutrition during my early years and youth. My parents were doers, not readers, and there were few books in our house. The Bible was there, but I didn't understand that it was great literature as well as Holy Writ, and didn't read it when I was young.

On the whole, I'm glad that I grew up in the country, but I can't help wishing I'd had the library experience that most of my friends, and nearly all writers, have enjoyed. Donna Tartt, in her book *The Little Friend*, writes feelingly, through her protagonist, of the way her hometown library sustained her. The opportunity to learn and the thrill of discovery are in libraries.

Now, when my car is being worked on in town, I usually go to the Judson library to wait. I start with the periodicals and literary quarterlies, and several hours later when I look up, the car is ready and I leave with regret. I hope, within a few months, to have more free time and to spend some of it in the nearby libraries, those wonderful resources that we often fail to support, don't use to full advantage, and often take for granted.

In the spring of 2003, Rick took me to Chattanooga, Tennessee, to receive the Hillsdale Award by the Fellowship of Southern Writers. I was happy to meet writers I'd known and admired from afar, Louis D. Rubin Jr., George Garrett, Elizabeth Spencer, Ellen Douglas, Bobbie Ann Mason, Jill McCorkle, Allan Gurganus, among others.

But that night I fell in my hotel room and made a hairline crack in a pelvic bone. It didn't show in the X-ray taken there, but I couldn't walk or stand.

So Rick, never losing either his patience or his cool, brought me home, propped up in the front seat beside him, to the Perry County Nursing Home where we were met by KW. A follow-up bone scan in Tuscaloosa showed the crack (a *pubic ramus* fracture). Surgery was not required, but I had to be in the nursing home again for five weeks of healing and therapy. Back at home, Home Help nurses and therapists came for five more weeks. So I recovered, but have never walked as well as before.

The down side of writing for writers like me is that there's so little time for reading. I don't know about other writers, but while I'm writing I don't read much. All of my energy goes into the work. When a work day is over, I feel the need to walk, move, clear my brain.

Still, like a miser, I go on collecting books. In every room the shelves are full. They're stacked on the floor, on benches and chairs. Sometimes, with a full day ahead, even a looming appointment, I'll glance at a book on a shelf and can't resist taking it down, if only to look at the page of contents.

The last speech that I wrote was the one I read at both the Mobile and Hoover libraries. Since I shortened it somewhat for Hoover, I'll end this memoir with that one.

Feb. 22, 2003

Since this conference is a project of the Hoover Public Library and since you're all probably readers, I'd like to tell you about my own books.

It would be pretentious to call my books a library, because it would give the wrong impression. You'd think of a large room in a big house. My house is modest. The rooms are small, and the books are not in one room but in every room. By now they've overflowed all the bookcases added year after year, until no wall space is left. The overflow is being stacked temporarily, I like to think, in front of the bookcases on the floor. When I know company is coming, I dust and restack them neatly, until the next time. I should be ashamed to tell you this, but I will. Some are stacked under my bed.

When I wake up in the morning in my bed, I see books wherever I look. Years ago, on the entire wall to my right, I had two large bookcases built to within a few inches of the ceiling. In that top space, stacked flat so that no space is wasted, are books too tall to fit in the shelves.

The bookcase on my right, closest to my bed and closest to my heart, houses books on the short story. My favorite short story writers are there, fixed stars like Chekhov, Flannery O'Conner, Ernest Hemingway, and the Russian-Jewish writer Isaac Babel. Babel fell victim to the Stalinist purges of 1930 and was killed before his work became widely known and appreciated. Joyce's *Dubliners* is there, and the stories of Katherine Anne Porter. Raymond Carver is there, but I don't go back and reread his stories as I do those of the fixed stars. Alice Munro and William Trevor will probably wind up there. Other favorites come and go. Some who were once there are now down on the floor. There are anthologies, mainly *The Best American Short Stories*, and books on usage (Fowler and Follett), dictionaries on slang, literary terms, and one titled *You All Spoken Here*, described as "a plunder room of words and phrases . . . used in southern parts of the United States." There are books on craft, technique, and criticism, mainly in paperback college textbooks picked up at book sales, which continue to help me understand and write short fiction.

On the top shelf of the adjoining bookcase are favorite novels, *War and Peace, Anna Karenina*, the novels of Faulkner, and a new icon of mine, Cormac McCarthy. *Madame Bovary* is there, *The Brothers Karamazov, Moby Dick, A Farewell to Arms*, and *Mrs. Bridge* by Evan S. Connell. The next shelf down holds favorite biographies and autobiographies, such as Isak Dinesen's *Out of Africa* and Alfred Kazin's *A Lifetime Burning in Every Moment.*

Down a shelf are collections of letters, among them the letters of Carl Jung, the psychoanalyst. In 1933 a Frau V. wrote Dr. Jung asking how one ought to live. What Dr. Jung replied has helped and/or confused me many times over the years. "There is no single, definite way for the individual which is prescribed for him and would be the proper one," Dr. Jung wrote back. "If you always do the next thing that needs to be done, you will go most safely and sure-footedly along the path prescribed by your unconscious." In other words, do the next most necessary thing. Which is in direct opposition to Joseph Campbell's famous counsel to "follow your bliss."

On the next two shelves, for no reasonable reason, are Greek and Roman classics, *The Iliad, The Odyssy, The Aeneid*, and the Theban plays. There's a group on folklore, including several by Zora Neale Hurston. Then, since I'm a jazz aficionado, there are biographies of jazz artists like Billie Holiday, Charlie Parker, and my favorite, Thelonious Monk. On the last shelf are poets, mainly Yeats, Eliot, Hopkins, and Christina Rossetti. Poets like Wallace Stephens and John Asbury I can't understand, so they're there only in anthologies.

My best literary friend for many years, the late Crawford Gillis, a Selma artist, had read everything worth reading in literature. He wasn't keen on contemporary literature, but since I am, he read the books I bought, or found, so we could talk about them. On his tombstone, he said he wanted engraved, "He returned books," which he did, punctiliously.

Anyway, one day after the two big book cases were built and

filled completely, he looked at them and said, "Are those bookcases nailed to the wall?" I'd never thought about it.

"Why?" I said.

"There was a writer," he said, and named an obscure writer of whom I'd never heard, "whose bookcase fell on him and killed him."

Well, I examined the bookcases and they were not nailed to the wall, just standing up on their own. I didn't really believe they'd fall on me, but the thought made me nervous. I asked my son to check them and he assured me that they were steadied by the contents and would never fall except in a tornado.

Still, some nights or mornings when I'm in bed feeling nervous and anxious in general, I look at those bookcases and wonder. If I should meet death by books, it might not be entirely inappropriate.

On the other side of my bed is an old homemade bench, about five feet long, stacked with two rows of books. The back row, held up by bookends, holds books on writing by the masters, *Ernest Hemingway on Writing, Robert Frost on Writing, Stephen King on Writing.* There's one titled *The Eye of the Story* by Eudora Welty. They're my "how-to" books, I guess you could say.

On the front row on the bench, stacked flat, are books I want to read, mean to read, and hope to read someday. Milton's *Paradise Lost* has been there for a long time (I don't know how I missed it in school, since I was an English major), but Donna Tart's *The Little Friend* didn't stay a day. Others I've read in part, and will finish in time, such as a collection of stories by Alistair MacLeod of Nova Scotia, titled simply *Island.* His stories are so good they have the power to inflict wounds and affect moods that last for days. To read one is almost like living through a challenging time in real life. So I have to space them out and read one when I feel *up* to it.

On the other side of the bench is a small bookcase, jammed

against my bill-paying desk, not my writing desk, which is back in my workroom. On one side of my dresser is a metal turning rack from some junk store. I don't know what it held originally, but now it's stuffed with books. Another tall but narrower bookcase, almost to the ceiling, stands behind the bedroom door, and books are stacked on the floor in front of it. The door to my bedroom won't open all the way back, because it's stopped at a right angle by books stacked behind it.

Almost everyone who comes into my bedroom, and all bookish visitors do, will sooner or later look at all the bookcases and say, "Have you read all these books?"

I have to tell the truth and shame the devil. I have not. I've read a good many, and a good many more I haven't. I no longer even hope to read them all, but I do hope to read *at* them as long as I can see.

One problem I've solved, after a fashion. When I read a book that I like, I want to underline favorite lines, paragraphs, or applaud the right word in the right spot, so I'll be able to go back and find it. I have a friend who draws little hearts in the margins by her favorite passages. Hearts are what I feel too, but underlining comes more naturally. I don't like to mark up nice editions, however. So I have Faulkner's books in The Library of America editions that just sit in glory on that top shelf, and paperback editions that I read and mark up. I have two sets of Chekhov, the Oxford University hardback edition on the shelf and the Ecco Press set in paperback, which I keep shut up in the box it arrived in. These I mark, as inconspicuously as possible, then put carefully back in the pasteboard box. I count on their being ready to go to the nursing home with me!

So we've been through only one room upstairs, and there's still my workroom, a guestroom now known as my granddaughters' room, since I no longer have overnight guests, and a sleeping porch, all full of books. About the books, I'm like a miser with his gold. On rare days when I have a few loose minutes, I like to simply look over the shelves, or get down on the floor and see what's there. Since none of the books are catalogued, and since as they have increased my memory has declined, this can be full of surprises.

One day, back around Thanksgiving I noticed several books by a critic, Lionel Trillin, who died in the seventies. I'd never looked inside those books since I put them there, so I took one out and saw a chapter titled "Flaubert's Last Testament." I love Flaubert because of *Madame Bovary* and that transcendent long short story, "A Simple Heart," and for his lifelong dedication to the art of writing. The essay was about his novel, *Bouvard and Pecuchet*, which I'd never read. I knew I had the book, because my friend Crawford, mentioned earlier, had read it. When I bought it, I remembered that he'd said he'd like to look at it again and took it home. In my mind I could see it, a thick, new book in a black binding. But I couldn't find it. For days, at least a week, in every spare minute I looked obsessively through books in all the rooms, including stacks on the floor.

Finally, I decided that for once in his life, Crawford hadn't returned a book. Then I took one more look, with a flashlight, in the place it should have been with everything else by and about Flaubert, in my workroom. On the top shelf of that bookcase, which is made from old pine shelving from my father's country store, with zigzag ends so the shelves can be adjusted, I looked again with the flashlight. Up on the top shelf is the Yale set of Shakespeare, a gift from my son Kirtley during his first job as a lawyer, and they take up most of the shelf. But down at the far end, I saw with the flashlight two faded old red books from some Goodwill or junk store, that I didn't recognize at all. I had to take them down to read the title. And that was the novel, in two volumes, the pages now brown around the edges. So I read it and am glad I did.

The sleeping porch on the south side of the house, all windows on three sides, was added by my parents after the house was built. At the time, it was thought healthful, a passing fad, I suppose, to sleep with windows wide open, winter and summer. So we slept out there under mounds of quilts, and blankets made from the wool of our own sheep, until I was moved into a room of my own. So the sleeping porch has only one wall of books.

But my first editions are out there. The two most notable are a hardback copy in excellent condition of *Stride Toward Freedom* by Martin Luther King, signed "Best wishes, Martin Luther King," which I bought in the Selma Salvation Army store for either a quarter or fifty cents, so long ago I can't remember which. The other is an example of poetic justice. When *To Kill a Mockingbird* was first published, I sent a copy as a gift to my brother-in-law, Roberts Brown, a lawyer in Opelika, who was a great reader. Years later when he died, childless and remarried, most of his books, including that one, came to me.

My workroom, which was my son's old bedroom, is like my own bedroom now, maybe worse, with two big bookcases, small bookcases between every stick of furniture, and books on the floor. But the books in one of the bookcases are mostly big volumes, often illustrated, such as *The Arabian Nights, The Last Days of Pompeii,* and *Don Quixote*, books to *have,* to *have* read, or to take down and look through, rather than to read. I should say here that I've seldom paid the steep, original price for such books. I found most of them at Ivy League university book-outs or from a Strand bookstore sale, by mail. One big book that I was recently glad to pay the full price for, however, is the King James Bible, designed and illustrated with engravings by Barry Moser.

Also back there are signed and unsigned copies of books by friends and acquaintances, including many fellow Alabamians, whom you know. Among those are books by the late Fred Bonnie, who wrote fine short stories, died far too young, and never got his literary due, in my opinion. Back there are also books that I keep as a southerner, in a South greatly changed since they were written: *Lanterns of the Levee, The Last of the Whitfields, With a Southern Accent, Stars Fell on Alabama. I'll Take My Stand* should be back there too, but is now in my granddaughter's room, in a glass-front bookcase from the Marion law office of my late half-brother, Sheldon Fitts. Brother, as I called him, lived down the road from me and is still sadly missing in my life.

And the dictionaries are there. My favorite, the one I use most, is *The American Heritage Dictionary*, third edition, because it's most up-to-date and has hundreds of pictures. There's now a fourth edition with the pictures in color, and I have it too, downstairs. Years ago, during lean years on the farm, my husband and son gave me for Christmas one year a wonderful surprise—*Webster's Third New International Dictionary*—unabridged, on a stand, and I still use it. I also have the *Compact Edition of the Oxford English Dictionary* which has to be read with a magnifying glass that came with it. I don't use it often, since I'm not a scholar and don't work the *New York Times* crossword puzzles every week as one friend does!

Also in my work room, behind my blueberry blue iMac, on what was called a "watermelon bench" when I bought it, are what I think of as writing props, Roget's and Webster's thesauruses, Webster's dictionary of synonyms. On the other side are *The New York Times Manual of Style and Usage* and *The Chicago Manual of Style*. On top of my desk is that tiny, well-known writer's bible, *The Elements of Style* by Strunk and White.

With all these books and helps and props, you'd think I could write beautiful, eloquent prose. Instead, I seldom use a word that I wouldn't be comfortable using in ordinary speech. I think I'm afraid it would be somehow out of character, so I look hard for simple words that are not clichés. And I spend half my writing time looking things up, trying not to make a mistake. Writing fiction is like writing nonfiction. Use one detail that's not true or right, and you lose your reader's trust. Sometimes forever.

When I brought you on this book tour of my house, we came straight upstairs to my bedroom. But there are books downstairs too. In the living room bookcases, on either side of the fireplace, are mostly sets, some from someone's once-fine library that wound up in an antique shop or even junk store. In those bookcases there's also a number of leather-bound books from a series of 100 American classics published by the Franklin Mint, in celebration of the American Revolution Bicentennial, and the Heritage Club books I began to buy the one year I worked at Judson before I married Kirtley.

When I was young, my favorite diversion was to rummage through second-hand bookstores, thrift stores, junk stores, and antique shops, looking for books. Many of the books that I have were found that way. Now, to find books that I can afford, I don't use the internet, the best place to find bargains, I know, because I'm afraid to give up my credit card information. So I use mainly two sources. Edward R. Hamilton, Bookseller, in Falls Church, Connecticut, by mail, and Daedalus Books in Columbia, Maryland, by phone. Both these sources are also on the internet.

But since books are my worst extravagance (I don't travel, dine out, or go to movies, and haven't had a vacation in twenty-five years), I often pick up the phone and order from my friends the independent booksellers.

So when do I read, after keeping a house and yard halfway pre-

sentable, looking after the farm (which is leased but still my responsibility, and also my *living*), and trying to be a tolerable mother and
grandmother? I always read in the morning, with a book propped
in front of me while I eat breakfast, and I'm always surprised how
fast I get from page 1 to page 300 that way. And I always read in
bed at night. Except for the noon and nightly news, I watch very
little television, often a real loss. I recently missed *The Forsyte Saga*,
again. But if I have to choose, read or watch, I usually read, unless
it's something like Ken Burns's Civil War or 9/11.

And when do I write? I haven't written a line of fiction since *It
Wasn't All Dancing* was published. To write fiction, I have to have
ahead of me a cleared-out space for sustained, full-time work. I
don't seem to be able to write an hour here, an hour there, as some
writers can, successfully. I can revise piecemeal but, so far, I haven't
been able to get a story down that way.

About a good workday for a writer, Eudora Welty said it best
in a little book titled *The Writer's Desk*: "I like to wake up ready to
go," she wrote, "and to know that during that whole day the phone
wouldn't ring, the doorbell wouldn't ring—even with good news—
and that nobody would drop in. This all sounds so rude. But you
know, things that just make a normally nice day are not what I
want. . . . I'd just get up and get my coffee and an ordinary breakfast
and get to work. And just have the whole day." I hope to have some
days like that after April of this year.

I don't read much when I'm writing, except things like the *Selma
Times-Journal* and *Time* magazine. Instead, I iron washed linens
that I've put up out of sight for months, clean out a closet, or walk
around my yard several times for exercise. Do mindless, physical
things. But I'm so happy when I'm working. It's the hardest thing
I've ever done, but the one I love most.

My greatest problem when writing fiction has always been deciding the next thing that needs to be done. There are duties, needs, and opportunities all around us. William Butler Yeats wrote a poem titled "All Things Can Tempt Me From This Craft Of Verse."

When I was writing the stories in *Tongues of Flame*, nobody, including me, thought that what I wrote would ever be worth the effort, so I was thought to be deluded and was generally let alone. When "The Amaryllis" was published in *McCall's* and a newspaper reporter tried to find me, he was told that I was something of a recluse. It hurt my feelings, because I've never wanted to shut myself away from the people or the life around me. But to write, one does have to somehow be shut away. In bed every night, I think of people I haven't stayed in touch with, letters and emails I haven't answered, opportunities I've let go by, even flowers I haven't put on the graves of my family.

I just hope I'll be able to write one or two more stories before I leave this earth and, at the same time, be forgiven a few sins of omission while I'm doing it.